Thanks for all your support over the years - can't believe it's over - oh well!! It's been fun, eh?!

All the best - Ellen + Chris Britchford

cebrit@yahoo.com

Great knowing you bott. Anytime you are in New Mexico Give us a call. 5054342151 Jo, thanks for all the advise, flubus!

Paulette + Chet

MAKE sure we keep in touch - ...dancing ...dy

Best of Leeck for a great future - thank you for all the great dancing over the years - Amal

amalayache@yahoo.com

Best of Luck. It's been great dancing with you.

Richard Hosler

rrhosler66@hotmail.com

OCTOBER 5, 2003

"DESERT DIAMONDS"

AL KHOBAR, SAUDI ARABIA

Richard + Jo
x4

The Story of the Eastern Province of Saudi Arabia

THE Story OF The Eastern Province OF SAUDI ARABIA

WILLIAM FACEY

STACEY INTERNATIONAL
LONDON

The Story of the Eastern Province of Saudi Arabia by William Facey

Published by Stacey International, 128 Kensington Church Street London W8 4BH

Editors: **Jill Waters** and **Kitty Carruthers**   *Art Director:* **John Fitzmaurice**

© Stacey International, 1994, 2000

British Library Cataloguing-in-Publication Data
A catalogue record for this book is available from the British Library.

ISBN 1 900988 18 6

Set in Sabon Roman Linotronic 11 on 13 point by SX Composing Limited, Rayleigh, Essex, England

Colour origination, printing and binding by Tien Wah Press, Singapore

Principal photographers: present day colour pictures **Mohammed Shabeeb**;
historical black-and-white pictures **Ilo Battigelli**.

Illustrations reproduced by kind permission of the following:
(*c = centre, l = left, r = right, b = bottom, t = top*)

Colour

Department of Antiquities: 22, 23, 24(2), 26(3), 27(3), 33, 34, 35(3), 36, 37(2), 39, 50, 52*b*; Saudi
Aramco: 9, 90, 94*t*, 113*b*, 121, 122(2), 123(2), 124(2), 125(2), 127, 128*cl*, 130*r*, 131*t&cl*, 144*l*, 152*cr*,
154*b*, 156(2); Colorific: 1, 108*b&c*, 115*tl*; William Facey: 10, 11,13*r*,14*tl*, 18, 40, 53(2), 55, 70*tr*, 71*t*,
79*cr*, 80*tr&bl*, 89*h*, 151(2), 152(*tl&bl*); John Grainger: 7, 12/13, 14*r&b*, 15*r*, 155*t*; Harrison Museum:
19*t&b*; Robert Harding: 110*bl*; Thor Heyerdahl: 28; H Jungius: 20; Geoffrey King: 48; Michael
McKinnon: 151, 153(2), 154(*t3*); Gulf Meridien: 112*b*; Ali Mubarak: 21, 44, 70*bl*, 81*b*, 82, 83(2), 85*b*,
109 *main*, 114*br*, 115*tr&br*, 119, 146*l*, 147*t*, 148 *main*, 150*t*; Royal Commission for Jubail and
Yanbu: 2/3, 4/5, 16, 114*l*, 118*b*, 126*b*, 135*cl*, 136/7(2), 138/9(4), 140/141(3), 142*c&b*, 155*br*; Al
Rushaid: 109*tr*, 118*tl*; 134*br&bl*, 135*bl*, 142*t*; Sabic: 102; Samarec: 112*t*, 126*t*, 130*l*,131*r*; Peter
Sanders: 87*b*, 110*tl&br*, 111, 113*tl&r*, 116, 117*t*, 118*tr*; Saudi Arabian Airlines: 143*b*; SCECO:
144*r&b*, 145(2), 146*c*; Mohammed Shabeeb: 70*tl*, 72, 87*t*, 104/5, 198*tl&tr*, 109*tl*, 110, 111*t*, 117*b*,
128/9, 132, 133, 135, 135*t*, 143*t*, *r&c*, 146*b*, 147 *main*, 148*tl*, 149(3), 150*bl*, 152*b*,155*b*; Ahmad Al-
Towaijri, (Amarat Madinat Al-Riyadh): 103, 106, 111(2), 155*b*; Roger Webster: 171, 65*t*;
Al-Zamil Group: 134*tl&tr*, 135*br*.

Black-and-white

Unless listed below, photographs were taken by Ilo Battigelli.

Saudi Aramco: 72*t*, 76*tl*, 79*b*, 81*t*, 91, 92*t*(2), 93*t*(2), 98, 99(2), 101; Sir Percy Cox (RGS):* 56/7, 86*b*;
J B Mackie (RGS): 75*t*; Joe Mountain (Saudi Aramco): 17*r*, 54, 86*t*, 95(2); H St J B Philby (RGS): 72*b*;
G Rendel (RGS): 60, 80*b*; A Rihani: 61*r*; W H I Shakespeare (RGS): 58/9(2), 61*tl*; Max Steineke (Saudi
Aramco): 19*tr*, 701*br*, 75*b*, 77*b*, 84, 92*b*, 93*b*, 94*b*.

———————————————————————————————

*RGS = Royal Geographical Society

Maps, diagrams and other illustrations

Chester Beatty Library, Dublin: 52*t*; J Crawford Fraser: 32; H R P Dickson, Unwin Hyman Ltd:
75; Pierpont Morgan Library, New York: 51*r*; F S Vidal/Arabian American Oil Company: 72.

CONTENTS

The publishers gratefully acknowledge help from the following organisations:
SCECO; Al Rushaid Group and Al-Zamil Group.
Special thanks to Saudi Aramco and the Royal Commission for Jubail and Yanbu,
whose support proved invaluable in the preparation of this book.

HRH Prince Muhammad ibn
Fahd ibn 'Abd al-'Aziz,
Governor of the Eastern
Province

Introduction

I T IS a mere half-century since oil was discovered in Saudi Arabia's Eastern Province. That discovery, and those that have followed, have turned the country into the world's largest oil producer. The region has drawn in thousands of technicians, labourers, businessmen, and experts in a vast range of fields, from all over the world, as well as from Saudi Arabia itself.

First impressions, particularly of an unfamiliar terrain and climate, are often misleading: it is difficult to overcome the feeling that existence here is possible only by virtue of one of the world's more spectacularly well organised triumphs of technology over harsh natural conditions.

The visitor travels in air-conditioned cars from his glittering hotel to air-conditioned office, along four-lane highways. Surrounding him, the apparently inhospitable desert is now interspersed with fine new urban estates and industrial office complexes with all that modern technology can provide. Though in the midst of aridity, he will be struck by an abundance of water that keeps parks and central reservations lush and green. New hospitals, sports facilities, schools and one of the finest technical universities in the world contribute to a picture in which everything seems to be possible, albeit by sustained and massive expenditure. For immediately beyond the perimeters of habitation, the environment of unaided nature, apparently waterless and barren, seems implacable – shimmering, distant and hostile.

Yet what has been happening in the Eastern Province in the second half of our century is the latest in a series of remarkable episodes in the long history of man's activities in the region, reaching back to the roots of ancient civilisation.

That said, the decades since the historic oil strike at Dammam Well no.7 in 1938 have witnessed the transformation of the Eastern Province, and with it the entire Kingdom of Saudi Arabia. The Eastern Province sits on the most extensive oil reserves anywhere in the world. Wisely used, they will ensure both the Kingdom's place as a major player in the global economy and its prosperity for the foreseeable future.

That oil resources bring riches to their owners is a commonplace of today's energy-hungry world. But the notion of prosperous societies having flourished in eastern Arabia in pre-modern times comes as a surprise to many. How can we account for the emergence of the civilisation of Dilmun in the third millennium BC, the rise of the legendary "lost city" of Gerrha in Classical antiquity, or the lightning successes of the Qarmatian rulers of Hasa Oasis in the early Middle Ages?

Throughout the story of the Eastern Province, four fundamental factors have been at work: its geographical location; the interplay of the nomads with the settled people of the coast and oases; the sea; and its fresh water resources.

Ancient Arabia as a whole profited from its geographical location between the great centres of civilisation. Though much of the Peninsula formed a barren immensity, to the south lay the Yemen and the Indian Ocean, and to the north the Fertile Crescent and Mediterranean centres of demand. In what would otherwise have been a region largely of marginal subsistence, its people were able to exploit trading opportunities.

Eastern Arabia, moreover, adjoins one of the ancient "cradles of civilisation". Call it Sumer, Babylonia, Mesopotamia or Iraq,

The Rub'al-Khali or Empty Quarter, which bounds the Eastern Province to the south, is the largest continuous sand desert in the world.

the "Land of the Two Rivers" (the Tigris and Euphrates) has been a powerful force in the history of the Eastern Province, whether by the land route or the sea. Not least, it has been throughout the millennia a magnet for trade, up the Gulf from the Indian Ocean, and across eastern and southern Arabia from the Yemen.

At different periods this trading activity brought great prosperity and cultural enrichment to Arabia. In such times, the incentive to settle could become imperative. Agricultural settlements developed into substantial caravan towns; their economic dominance brought in its train a shift of political and military power to the settled rulers as distinct from the nomadic tribes to whom, at other times, power reverted. In this way life in Arabia has responded to a rhythm of power alternating between the nomads and the settled people, with the attractions of the oasis and coastal settled areas continually providing an incentive to the nomads to settle, and sometimes to become involved in the larger process of state formation.

The Gulf, so important today as a commercial waterway, has experienced several previous periods of outstanding prosperity. Indeed, it can claim to be the most ancient long-distance sea-way used by man. Throughout history, the coast has exerted a cosmopolitan, outward-looking influence on the hinterland of eastern Arabia, bringing not only trade goods but influxes of people, new practices, ideas and technologies into the region, influencing to varying degrees the tribal settlers and nomads beyond.

The sea has also provided food, as well as another important resource: pearls. Pearl fishing has a long history in the Gulf and, before oil, the trade in pearls was the mainstay of the economies of the Arab maritime states of the Gulf.

Finally, belying its apparently remorseless aridity, this part of eastern Arabia sits upon vast reserves of fresh water. By the lift of the earth's crust, the waters of ancient Arabia during earlier geological epochs have drained into the aquifers – at different depths – of today's eastern Arabia. Some of these aquifers break surface in copious natural artesian springs, creating the great oases of al-Hasa, Qatif and Bahrain.

Here the lush surroundings have always provided a sharp contrast with the deserts around, and have been the setting for a history of continuous settlement and agriculture which reaches back to Neolithic times. This natural abundance is thought to have given rise to the name which was once used to denote all this part of eastern Arabia, al-Bahrain. Now the name of the islands alone, Bahrain means "the two seas" – thought to be an ancient reference to the salt sea of the surface and the freshwater "sea" beneath.

The development of the Eastern Province demanded the services of foreigners from all over the world. From the early 1980s the expatriate population began to recede as a highly educated Saudi workforce became available to take on a wide range of skills and responsibilities. The Eastern Province remains a region in rapid transition, symbolised most dramatically by the creation of the new industrial city of Jubail on the Gulf coast – a flagship of the Kingdom's policy to diversify the scope and location of its economy and to expand the role of private enterprise.

In this surge of development, in a region of such vital significance, it is all too easy in today's Eastern Province to overlook the past – to fail to acknowledge the part that the history and culture of a place must play in the present. This book aims to present the reader not only with the contrast between past and present but also, by highlighting continuities with the past, with an enriched understanding of the region today.

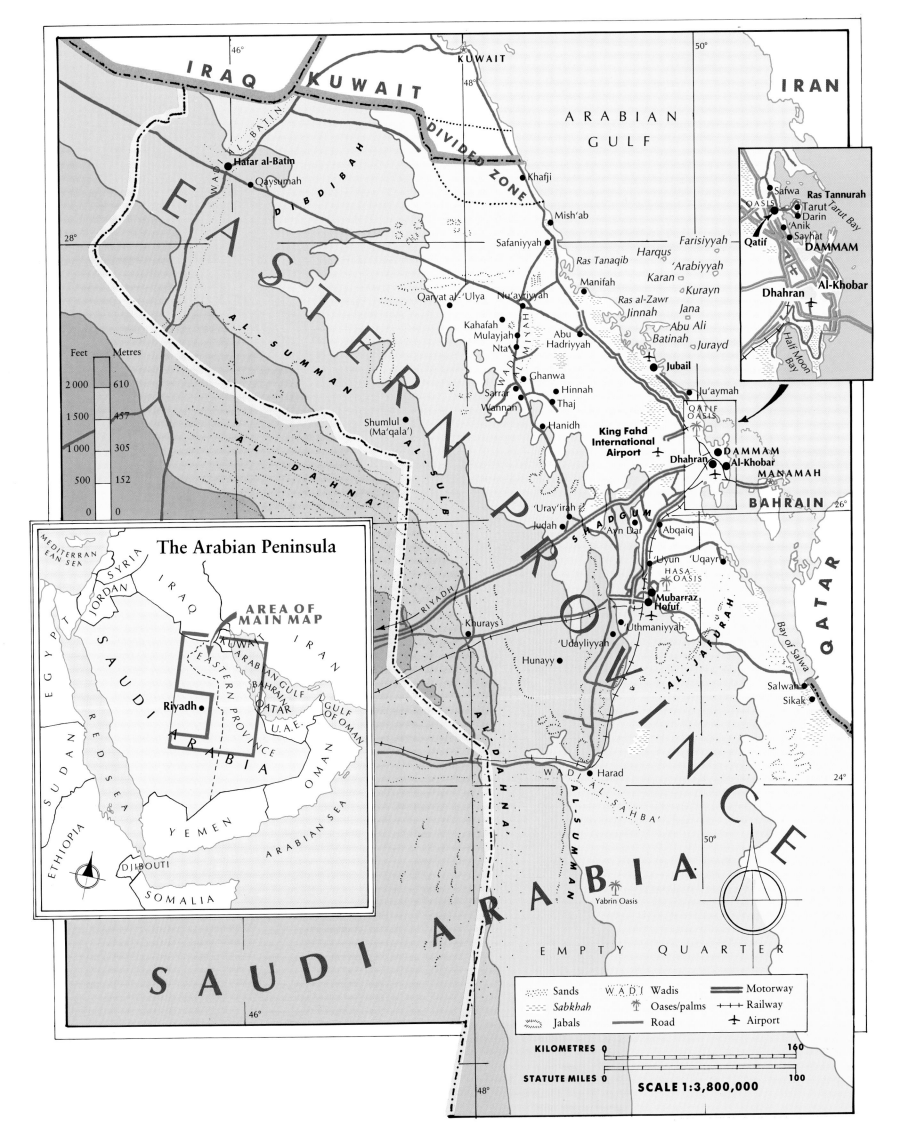

IRAQ KUWAIT KUWAIT IRAN

ARABIAN
GULF

46° 48° 50°

Hafar al-Batin
Qaysumah

DIVIDED ZONE

Khafji

Mish'ab

Safaniyyah

Farisiyyah

Harqus
Ras Tanaqib *'Arabiyyah*
Manifah *Karan*
Qaryat al-'Ulya Nu'ayriyyah *Ras al-Zawr Kurayn*
Jinnah Jana
Kahafah *Abu Ali*
Mulayjah Abu *Batinah Jurayd*
Nta' Hadriyyah
Jubail
Ghanwa Ju'aymah
Satrar Hinnah
Wannan Thaj QATIF
OASIS
Shumlul Hanidh **King Fahd
(Ma'qala')** **International
Airport**
Dhahran **DAMMAM
Al-Khobar**
MANAMAH
'Uray'irah
Judah SHADGUM BAHRAIN 26°
Ayn Dar Abqaiq
'Uyun 'Uqayr
HASA
OASIS
**Mubarraz
Hofuf**
Khurays Uthmaniyyah
'Udayliyyah
Hunayy
Salwah
Sikak
Harad
50°
24°

EASTERN PROVINCE

WADI AL-BATIN DIBDIBAH AL-SUMMAN AL-SULB AL-DAHNA' WADI AL-MIYAH RIYADH AL-DAHNA' AL-JAFURAH Bay of Salwa QATAR

28°

EMPTY QUARTER

SAUDI ARABIA

WADI AL-SAHBA' AL-SUMMAN
Yabrin Oasis

Inset: Eastern Province (top right)
Safwa **Ras Tannurah**
OASIS Tarut Tarut Bay
Darin
Anik
Sayhat
Qatif **DAMMAM**
Dhahran **Al-Khobar**
Half Moon
Bay

Inset: The Arabian Peninsula (left)
MEDITERRANEAN SEA
SYRIA
JORDAN IRAQ IRAN
EGYPT **AREA OF
MAIN MAP**
KUWAIT
ARABIAN GULF
BAHRAIN
SAUDI ARABIA QATAR U.A.E.
Riyadh EASTERN PROVINCE GULF OF OMAN
RED SEA OMAN
SUDAN ARABIAN SEA
ETHIOPIA YEMEN
DJIBOUTI
SOMALIA

Legend
Sands	W A D I Wadis	Motorway
Sabkhah	Oases/palms	Railway
Jabals	Road	Airport

Feet **Metres**
2 000 — 610
1 500 — 457
1 000 — 305
500 — 152
0 — 0

KILOMETRES 0 ————————— 160
STATUTE MILES 0 ————————— 100
SCALE 1:3,800,000

CHAPTER ONE

Landscape and Climate

The geological past

I MAGINE the Arabian Peninsula and the bed of the Gulf together as a tray, slightly tilted so that it is higher on the western side, and slopes gently down towards the east. The tray has a raised rim, but only on two sides, the western and southern, forming the mountain ranges of the Hijaz, Asir, Yemen and Oman.

The low, sloping eastern edge of this rectangle is lapped by the waters of the Arabian Gulf. And the edge is irregular, as the sea conceals the fact that the Arabian Peninsula is being gradually subducted, by tectonic forces, beneath the Iranian landmass. The same forces have pushed up and folded the mountain chain of the Zagros range and highlands of Iran. The mountains of western Arabia have been squeezed upwards as the Red Sea Rift widens, forcing Arabia away from Africa. Both the Arabian and Iranian mountains are formed of very ancient, pre-Cambrian (at least 600 million years old) rocks, whose composition has been altered by compression, heat and volcanic action.

Between these two ranges, Arabia's slight tilt has resulted in a shallow basin, today filled by the Gulf – the Tigris-Euphrates river system feeds into it – and the eastern coasts of the Arabian Peninsula as far as the mountains of Oman.

The Eastern Province occupies the eastern side of the Arabian Shelf, the strata of which are relatively young, dating from 230 million years ago. They were gradually laid down over the older rocks of the Arabian Shield, which are exposed only in Arabia's western half. Much of the Shelf is composed of limestone layers formed under shallow seas which, at various epochs, covered eastern and northern Arabia. It is in these seas, over millions of years, that the marine organisms were deposited which today form the oil reserves which have brought wealth to the states bordering the Gulf.

Eastern Province landforms

The Eastern Province forms the entire eastern portion of the Kingdom of Saudi Arabia. It is a strip roughly 200 kilometres wide, running from the Kuwait border in the north to the sands of the Rub ‘al-Khali, or Empty Quarter, in the south. Its Gulf shore, from Kuwait to Qatar, defines the northern part of its eastern boundary. In the west it is enclosed, as far south as the latitude of Yabrin, by the Dahna’ sands. The Dahna’ forms a natural barrier dividing the Eastern Province from Najd. It is an immense, fluid monument to the prevailing north-north-west winds of eastern Arabia. In a vast sweep about 80 kilometres wide and 1200 kilometres long, the Dahna’ joins the Nafud Desert in the north to the Empty Quarter in the south. Its high, pinky-brown dunes are longitudinal, lining up with the wind direction and known as *‘uruq* (sing. *‘irq*).

Unlike the scarps of Najd,

The vast palm groves of Hasa Oasis seen from Jabal Sha‘ban.

◀ A mature date palm garden in Hasa Oasis.

the Summan scarp, which is an ancient cliff forming the eastern edge of the Summan Plateau, faces east. It is mostly 20-30 metres high, but rises in places to 80 metres or more. The Summan Plateau extends in a long line which, in its centre, bulges eastwards towards Hasa Oasis. The bulge is called the Sulb Plateau. The eastern edge of the Summan and Sulb is eroded and broken into isolated jabals and small table-lands, capped by resistant rocks. The Shadgum Plateau, and Jabal Qarah in Hasa Oasis, are both isolated remnants of the Summan Plateau. The entire escarpment was once the cliff of a shallow sea which covered the region for long periods up until the middle of the Pliocene epoch some three million years ago. The wave-cut character of the rock outcrops can be seen most clearly in the gorges and caves of Jabal Qarah, which are now used for recreation by the people of Hasa Oasis, and on the sides of the Shadgum Plateau.

The Ghawar oil field, the largest onshore field in the world, was formed by the organisms laid down over millions of years by an ancient sea. It lies east of the scarp of the Summan and Sulb Plateaux, just west of Hasa Oasis. As the sea receded, it left a flat coastal plain with outcrops of limestone and sandy limestone which were survivors of the Summan Plateau. In some places near the coast, rocks of more ancient origin penetrate the recent strata. These dome formations, for example the Dammam dome, gave early geologists the clue to the oil that lay beneath the rock.

The Dahna' Sands, running along the centre of the Summan Plateau, are characterised by high, pinky-brown dunes.

Over the coastal plain, climatic forces can be seen in action today, as the wind blows the whitish sands of the Jafurah desert southwards from around the Jubail area. The Jafurah passes east of Hasa Oasis, and widens as it extends south, its low dunes moving visibly from year to year. Winter rains revive the perennial shrubs and bring life to annual seeds, and this type of vegetated, sandy terrain is known locally as *dikakah*.

In the north and south, two enormous flat gravel plains spread out over the coastal plain. They are triangular in shape, because they are the remains of two ancient deltas. The Dibdibah in the north is the fan formed by gravels washed down by the Wadi Batn, once the extension of the major river system which drained

Central Arabia, the relic of which in al-Qasim is called the Wadi Rimah. In the south, the Wadi Sahba' breaks through the Summan scarp near Harad. Once it was a major river draining southern Najd from Kharj, and the relic of its delta is the thin gravel fan which spreads out towards the Sabkhat Matti and the present-day shore.

At its southern end, the Dahna' sand strip merges into the Empty Quarter. Known locally simply as *al-rimal*, "the sands", it is the largest continuous sand desert in the world. In the north it is typified by barchan dunes, large sand masses in the form of crescents with their horns pointing downwind. In other areas dunes of *'irq* type are prevalent.

What we see today represents desert formation during several arid phases during the Pleistocene age, with wind-blown sands of recent hyper-arid centuries form-

The base of Jabal Qarah with its ancient, wave-eroded gorges and caves.

In the summer, the saline water of this drainage *sabkhah* (*above*) near Jawatha, Hasa Oasis, will evaporate to form the encrusted surface of a salt flat.

ing the top layer. Most of the actual material of the Empty Quarter – the sands – is in fact the product of water action: it is dried-out alluvium washed down from western and central Arabia by rivers which flowed during wet phases in the late Pliocene and early Pleistocene epochs – the last five million or so years. The major river courses broke through the Tuwayq chain in places that can still be seen: Wadi Hinu near Qaryat al-Faw, Wadi Dawasir and Wadi Nisah or Sahba'. At that time the Empty Quarter formed a low-lying deltaic basin, much of which had in previous ages been covered by sea.

The landscape along the coast is in places hardly above sea level. The slope of the shore is barely perceptible, often making it difficult to identify a precise shoreline. In such locations the ebb tide can expose an intertidal zone up to one kilometre wide, despite the difference between high and low tide along the Gulf coast averaging less than one and a half metres. This intertidal zone is a vital feeding-ground for birds and marine life, and the silts of Tarut Bay, enriched by drainage from Qatif Oasis and Tarut Island itself, are especially important.

The flat coastline is also typified by shallow saline lagoons and salt flats, known as *sabkhah*s. *Sabkhah*s originate either as enclosed lagoons evaporate out, or as water drawn up from under ground by capillary action, which draws up salts which then crystallise out due to evaporation. Around Hasa Oasis, the extensive *sabkhah*s are the

Typical *dikakah* sand and vegetation, in this case overlying the coastal *sabkhah* around 'Uqayr.

result of drainage from the irrigated areas. The *sabkhah*s near Half Moon Bay may well be the relics of the "river" or series of swamps which are thought once to have taken the excess waters of Hasa Oasis to the sea.

The coastal currents run chiefly from north to south, in the same direction as the prevailing winds. But much of the coastline lies in shallow, sheltered bays, where small volumes of water cover relatively large areas, disturbed only by weak currents. Extreme summer heat causes rapid evaporation and high levels of salinity; but the shallows support sea grass beds and, in water up to fifteen metres deep, coral reefs may grow. Both are important marine life nurseries and food sources. The coral reefs in places have built up into flat-topped platform reefs, against which sand has built up, leading eventually to the emergence of an island.

The Gulf is a relatively young sea. Very shallow on the Arabian side, it slopes down gently until it reaches its greatest depth – about 100 metres – on the Iranian side. It averages only 35 metres in depth. It is therefore a very small volume of water, which is exposed to intense solar radiation for much of the year, causing rapid evaporation leading to high salinity. Because its

Barchan dunes in the Empty Quarter.

Sand and *sabkhah* in the Empty Quarter (*opposite*) contrast dramatically with the richness of marine life off the coast of the Eastern Province.

volume is small, it is especially vulnerable to major pollution disasters such as the oil spill caused during the Iraqi occupation of Kuwait in 1990-1.

However, the Gulf supports a rich marine life, particularly in its shallows, where sea grass beds attract the rare dugong. Coral reefs grow between Safaniyyah and Abu Ali, and coral islands serve as breeding grounds for turtles.

The rich vegetation of the oases of al-Hasa and Qatif contrasts with the sparseness of the rest of the terrain in the Eastern Province. Natural artesian waters support the cultivation of vast palm groves, orchards, vegetable gardens, crops, and tamarisk and other trees. Alongside grows a variety of wild shrubby plant cover, annual plants, grasses and reed beds. Bird life is rich, especially as these oases lie on a major north-south migration route, and animal life flourishes, with such species as the Indian Grey Mongoose and Asiatic Jackal represented. Fish abound in the irrigation canals.

Since the Aramco compound was built at Dhahran in the 1940s and 1950s, with its gardens and landscaping, man-made environments have become an increasingly important feature of the Eastern Province scenery. With careful planning, landscaping and maintenance, the adverse environmental impact of industrial installations, land reclamation and coastal recreation projects can be minimised, and even turned to advantage. The Royal Commission for Jubail and Yanbu is developing salt-tolerant planting schemes to maximise the vegetation potential of hith-

Part of the man-made coastline at Jubail.

underground water-bearing strata of different depths and ages. The water which comes to the surface in the oases of al-Hasa and Qatif is held in the Alat, Khobar and Umm al-Radhuma formations. Since these strata are tilted slightly downwards towards the east, the water travels slowly, building up natural pressure, and finds outlets to the surface, through cracks and faults in the rock, east of the Summan escarpment. Today the rainfall of Arabia is insufficient to replenish these aquifers where they begin, and the water which is coming to the surface now has been estimated to be between 24,000 and 33,000 years old.

In the past the natural artesian water was more than sufficient to meet the needs of the population. In antiquity, for example in the third and first millennia BC, the flow of water seems to have been sufficient not only to sustain agriculture in Hasa Oasis but to create a flow, possibly a perennial one, to the Gulf shore in the vicinity of Half Moon Bay. Hasa Oasis itself seems to have been larger, and the coast north and south of Qatif more extensively populated and farmed. If this was the case, then since that time the flow has much diminished.

The increasing demand for water for industrial, agricultural and domestic use requires careful use of groundwater resources. The government has installed large desalination plants on the Gulf and

erto unpromising areas. Urban parks, central reservations on highways, irrigation schemes, sand stabilisation by planting, and even sewerage outfalls can provide more varied habitat for wildlife, particularly birds on migration.

Groundwater resources

The natural groundwater which comes to the surface in Hasa Oasis and Qatif originated in the distant past as rain falling in central Arabia. This rainfall seeps into

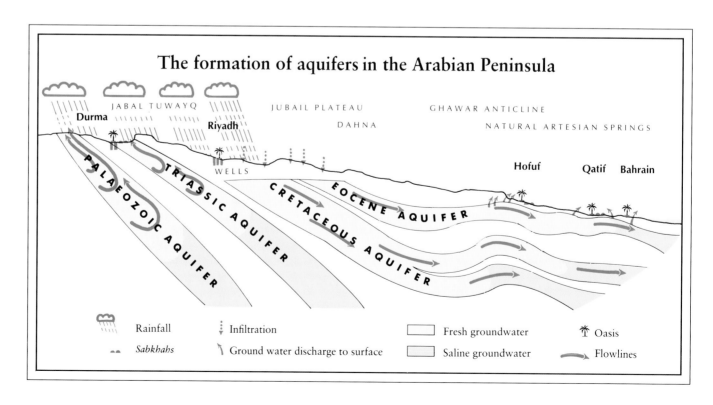

The formation of aquifers in the Arabian Peninsula

Al Murrah tribesmen draw water from a newly dug well on the edge of the Jafurah sands.

the great trans-continental river systems were eroded are thought to have occurred during the late Pliocene-early Pleistocene epoch – between one and a half and three and a half million years ago. The relics of these river systems in the Eastern Province are the Wadi Batn in the north, and the Wadi Sahba' in the south. Some of the abundant but very deep ground-water resources of Saudi Arabia date from this period. During the Pleistocene, wet and dry periods alternated, the last wet period occurring between 33,000 and 24,000 years ago, when wadi flow increased greatly, the aquifers which feed the oases were filled, and lakes were formed.

A period of increasing dryness followed, until 15,000 BC, after which exceptional aridity combined with strong winds prevailed up to about 8000 BC. This period was as arid as the present day, and during it the great sand areas of Saudi Arabia assumed the form which they have maintained until now.

A lesser wet phase characterised the Neolithic period. It lasted, on present evidence, between 8000 BC and 4000 BC, and favoured the development of the first permanent settlements. The limited shallow ground-water resources of the Kingdom date from this more recent period.

Since then, the climatic trend in Arabia has been towards greater aridity, possibly with two moister intervals. These are thought to have occurred towards the end of the first millennium BC and the early first millennium AD – the period of the great Arabian trading cities – and also during mediaeval times.

Red Sea coasts which convert sea water into fresh. Today Riyadh is supplied with potable water from Jubail through an 800-kilometre pipeline. Looking to the future, experiments with plants which will tolerate salt-water irrigation are also under way.

Climate in the past

It can come as a surprise to learn that the arid Saudi Arabian landscape we see today is chiefly the product of rainfall and water erosion. Yet this fact is obvious to anyone flying over the country: there is no vegetation to conceal the branching dry wadi systems which network across much of the terrain otherwise buried by sand and loess – the wind-born siliceous dust.

The major rainy periods during which

A freshwater well in the sea off al-Khobar, 1935.

Gulf sea levels

For millions of years before the Gulf as we know it today came into existence, the basin which includes eastern Arabia and the Tigris-Euphrates river system was covered by a shallow sea. During the Miocene period (25-12 million years ago), Arabia continued to swing slowly eastwards as the Red Sea rift opened up.

Investigations at Sarrar, west of Thaj in the Wadi al-Miyah, have revealed that a rich natural environment existed about 17 million years ago. This was a coastal estuarine area, though today it is 100 kilometres from the sea. Mangroves flourished in the hot and humid tropical climate, and there were mud-flats, lagoons and swamps. Streams bordered by palms drained the higher ground to the west. Here grassland supported ancestral forms of gazelle, giraffe, rodents and rabbits. Mastodons and rhinoceros roamed the savannah while Dryopithecus, ancestor of today's apes, inhabited the woodlands.

About five million years ago, the sea cut the cliff which today forms the Summan escarpment, and then retreated. A period of substantial rainfall followed which cut the wadi systems, bringing us into the Pleistocene period which began about two million years ago.

The Pleistocene is the epoch during which the Ice Ages occurred: up to twenty alternating periods of significantly colder and warmer climate are recognised. The theory is that, during an ice age, the polar ice caps locked up so much of the earth's water that a worldwide drop in sea level was caused.

Most is known about the last Ice Age; from the last interglacial about 120,000 years ago, the trend towards a colder climate continued until the glacial maximum in c.18,000 BC. This was almost certainly accompanied by a steady fall in Gulf sea-levels, albeit an erratic one. It is, however, generally accepted that there was a drop in sea level of about one hundred metres or more, which would have left the Gulf basin dry. The floor of the Gulf would have been a continuation of the Tigris-Euphrates system, with lagoons and marshes, and an estuary around the Straits of Hormuz. The rest of the land surface, perhaps with a residual vegetation after the earlier rains of 33,000-24,000 years

Yellow broomrape is a common parasite which draws its nutrients from the roots of other plants.

ago, would have dried out and become desertic as aridity set in around 15,000 BC. With the melting of the ice caps the Gulf gradually filled again, reaching today's level in about 6000 BC. By 4000 BC the level seems to have risen to about two metres above the present-day mark, before gradually falling back.

Evidence for man's occupation of the Eastern Province before 10,000 BC is lacking, possibly due to the high sea levels prevalent at times during the Early Palaeolithic. Nor are there Middle Palaeolithic finds from the period beginning around 100,000 years ago. However, with a dry Gulf during much of this period, man may have inhabited the estuarine country which is now covered by the sea. The first significant signs of human occupation seem to be relatively late – during the Neolithic period from c.5000 BC – but further research may change this picture.

Climate and seasons today

The Eastern Province lies within an arid climatic belt extending from the Atlantic in the west to Pakistan in the east, and including the Sahara. It experiences extreme heat and dryness in the summer, though its latitude is sufficiently far north for the four seasons to be distinguishable.

Lack of rain, clear skies and intense sunshine are typical of the long summer from May to September, and at times the dryness of the terrain can lead to dust storms. Virtually no rain at all falls during this period, and temperatures tend to be very high – 50°C has been recorded, and July and August averages are over 35°C. Inland, away from the moderating effect of the sea, the day-night temperature change can be considerable: 18°C in summer, and 11°C in winter. Averages for December and January, the coolest months, are around 15°C, but cloudless nights can occasionally be frosty. Relative humidity is low, except on the coast where it can be uncomfortably high. The dry north-westerly *shamal* is the prevailing wind of summer, but dies out during July to give a calm August.

From September the climate is increasingly dominated by the eastward-moving succession of depressions which cross northern Arabia from the Mediterranean,

The jerboa, one of the desert's most adaptable inhabitants, is nocturnal; it derives its moisture from succulent plants and dew.

The *dhabb* or spiny-tailed lizard is the most conspicuous of the desert's many reptiles. This one provided a diversion for some American geologists, c.1937.

most intriguing aspect of the flora and fauna is the ways in which species have adapted to survive.

The Eastern Province falls within the great Saharo-Arabian vegetation zone. Plants in this zone face many environmental problems – low rainfall, high temperatures, desiccating winds and saline soil. Yet some 360 species in all have been identified in the Eastern Province and, though sparsely distributed, the more common species were in the past sufficient to support a thinly distributed animal life, both wild and domesticated. The latter, in turn, supported a culturally adapted human population of nomadic pastoralists. The bedouin divide the plant world into *'ushb*, the tender annuals that flourish briefly after rain, and *shajar*, all the plants from shrublets to trees that are able to meet the harsh test of summer.

Many species of plant have evolved techniques to deal with aridity, heat and saline soil. The date palm, perhaps originally domesticated in eastern Arabia, tolerates high salinity and intense sunshine. Its domestication was the vital factor in the development of oasis agriculture, in which other crops, fruits and vegetables could be grown. The date palm, therefore, provided not only the staple food for the settled Arabian, but conditioned the nature of his settled existence, which revolved around its cultivation.

In other plants, taproots seek out deep

affecting the region as far south as the latitude of Ras Tannurah. October-November is a cooler transitional season during which this new weather pattern takes effect, and may be thought of as autumn. Winds become much more variable in direction, and rain may fall at any time from November to April, though it peaks usually in December and January, the two-month winter, during which localised storms and strong winds are not unusual and it can also be cold, even by day.

Rainfall is highest in the north of the region, decreasing as one goes south. This has an obvious impact on the grazing potential of the land. In the Empty Quarter, ten years may pass without any rain at all. Wherever it occurs, but more particularly the further south one goes, rain is sporadic and unreliable. It may be very heavy in one locality, missing others altogether. Rainfall averages are therefore misleading: while the regional annual average is about 75mm, typical annual amounts in any one place may vary from a mere 15mm to 150mm and more.

Plant and animal adaptations

The rains of winter and spring, which can be thought of as lasting from February to April, refresh the perennial plants and bring to life the annual plants and grasses upon which the nomadic bedouin used to rely for grazing. In a reversal of the norm in more temperate climes, annuals cope with the heat of summer, rather than the cold of winter, by reducing themselves to seeds. In this extreme environment, the

The Rhim gazelle, once common in the Eastern Province, survives on the edge of the Empty Quarter.

moisture, while a reduced leaf and stem surface area, and waxy or hairy leaf and stem coatings minimise water loss. Succulence and salt excretion are to be found among some perennials, while one common group of species is parasitic on the roots of other plants. The seeds of some annuals can lie dormant for years before germination, and at least one annual plant's seeds are thought to have evolved a type of staggered germination, so that they do not all grow, flower and wither at once. In this way the species maximises its chances of survival.

In the same way, many animals have adapted, both physically and in their habits, to cope with heat and aridity. Rodents and their predators escape the daytime heat by being nocturnal. Some rodents aestivate, the desert equivalent of hibernation, in deep burrows during the summer. The jerboas, gazelles and oryx can survive without free water, deriving their moisture from succulent plants and dew. Reptiles, such as the large Spiny-tailed Lizard, or *dhabb*, are similarly adapted. Large ears are common – for example in the Arabian Hare, Desert Hedgehog, Sand Rat and Desert Wolf – to facilitate heat loss. They also enable hearing over long distances, an important ability in a sparsely populated habitat. In general, desert species tend to be smaller, slenderer and longer-legged than members of the same species elsewhere – a physical adaptation which enables them to lose heat easily. Finally, many desert species tend to be lighter in colour than their cousins in other habitats, to merge with the colour of their surroundings.

Though no longer found in a truly wild state the camel, which in its single-humped form is probably native to Arabia, epitomises an animal adapted to desert existence. Its hump, long legs, feet, nose, eyelids, mouth and urinary system are all extreme physical adaptations to hot arid conditions. Its blood system allows it to tolerate a wider range of change in body temperature than any other mammal. In domesticating this highly mobile animal, Arabian man found a near-perfect solution to the problem of existence in his increasingly austere environment. Just as the development of oasis life was conditioned by the date palm, so the emergence of nomadism was intimately bound up with the domestication of the camel.

The long-eared Arabian Hare.

CHAPTER TWO

Origins

The Stone Age

THE EARLIEST abundant evidence of life in eastern Arabia belongs to the Neolithic period, some 7,000 years ago. It is likely that man had inhabited these parts before, but there is no evidence for this as yet.

The Pleistocene epoch closed with a period of aridity lasting from around 15,000 BC until 8000 BC. With the Holocene or Recent epoch which followed and continues to the present day, came the start of a period of modest increase in moisture. Datable marsh deposits from the Empty Quarter show that springs and shallow lakes had appeared, implying that eastern Arabia was markedly, if intermittently, more hospitable than today between c.8000 BC and 4000 BC. This period saw the emergence of Neolithic cultures with the first domesticated animals and plants over a wide area of the Middle East, from Egypt through the Fertile Crescent to Turkey, Iraq and the Zagros Mountains of Iran.

Keeping animals and growing crops transformed human society. Settlement, surplus production, trade and the development of a social hierarchy, led to the emergence of towns and cities.

In eastern Arabia, the hunters and gatherers slowly developed into cattle herders and harvesters of wild cereals. By c.5000 BC, they had encountered the Ubaid culture of Iraq, which brought to them the first pottery to be used in Arabia. Ubaid pottery of three different phases dating between 5100 BC and 3500 BC has been found on Eastern Province sites.

The earliest site lies inland at 'Ayn Qannas, just north of Hasa Oasis: a simple circular mud dwelling, with an enclosure of reeds or palm fronds. The top four excavated layers yielded fine pressure-flaked stone tools of developed Neolithic type, Ubaid pottery and cattle bones. The lower levels pre-date the Ubaid pottery and yielded stone blade-type tools typical of the early Neolithic hunters and gatherers.

Later sites lie near the coast to the north and south of Jubail where abundant Ubaid pottery, dated 4200-3400 BC, and fine stone tools have been found. The huge quantities of shells and fish bones show that these coastal people relied on the sea for food, and suggest that pearl-fishing traces its origins to this remote time.

These clues and others from the Gulf and Omani littoral also speak of wide-ranging contact by sea around the Peninsula, made by short coastal hops between settlements. Small craft fashioned out of the mid-ribs of palm fronds, like the surviving *shashah* (primitive fishing craft) of today, or from bundles of the *Phragmites* reed which is abundant on the coastal flats, would have been well within the technical capabilities of these late Stone Age people.

Dilmun – the first civilisation

The links between southern Iraq and the peoples of the

A carved male figure, in white limestone, of Sumerian type (c.2700 BC), found on Tarut Island. The statue is about a metre tall.

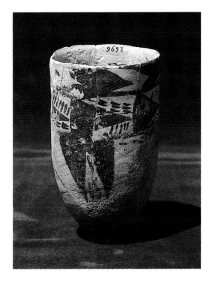

A reconstructed pot of Ubaid III type, found in the Eastern Province.

eastern Arabian coast endured beyond the Ubaid period. By 3000 BC Arabians were experiencing, for the first time, a form of urban civilisation of their own, thanks to Sumerian influence. The Sumerians had established a number of city states in southern Iraq, among them Ur. Today many miles inland, Ur is thought to have stood in those days on the shore of the Gulf. Sumerian civilisation – apparently an indigenous growth – is thought to be the most ancient of the great civilisations of antiquity, pre-dating even that of Egypt, over which it seems to have exerted some formative influences.

This immensely important period in Mesopotamia – the "Land of the Two Rivers" – and the Gulf had many of the hall-marks of the new urban societies growing up elsewhere in the Middle East: increasingly complex settlements grew into towns, together with their attendant centralisation of religion and trade, a developing social stratification, division of labour, evolving technology, a silver standard of exchange, and writing systems. We, today, are heirs of these processes, which the Sumerians are generally given the credit for developing.

The Sumerians themselves seem to have looked to eastern Arabia for their origins, at least in part. The region owed its increasing involvement in this sphere of influence to the growth of long-distance seafaring. Presumably building on the short-hop network of Neolithic times, it was possible to establish regular trade

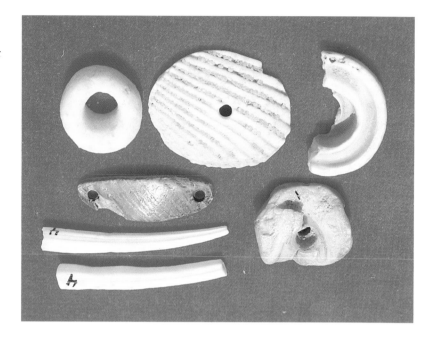

Shell artefacts pierced and worked by miniature stone awls, from coastal Ubaid sites.

contacts as far afield as Oman.

By the early third millennium BC Sumerian influence had become paramount on the coast of the Eastern Province. Tarut Island, just off Qatif, seems to have had a major settlement early on. Many fragments of exquisite workmanship of chlorite schist have come to light at the site of Rafi'ah on the island, and the sixteenth century Portuguese fort in the centre of the island probably stands over important remains of this period. Other finds from Rafi'ah include a fine male figure in limestone and a tiny figurine of a man in lapis lazuli, the nearest source of which is northern Pakistan; in addition pottery fragments have been found, thus demonstrating contacts with southern Iraq, the southern Gulf coast and the Indus Valley.

The earliest references to the land of Dilmun are nowadays taken to mean the mainland of the Eastern Province, including Tarut Island. Later, however, from 2450-1700 BC, the civilisation known as Dilmun developed with the island of Bahrain as its chief centre.

An impressive sequence of cities has been identified at Qal'at al-Bahrain on the island of Bahrain. By contrast, no large settlement sites have been located on the Arabian mainland. So far, the only settlement evidence comes from two small sites, Tell al-Ramad in Hasa Oasis, and Umm al-Nussi in Yabrin Oasis far to the south. The theory that the thriving port on Tarut would have stimulated the growth of oasis agriculture in both Qatif and Hasa Oasis is

Fine stone projectile points, scrapers and blades, together with quantities of fish bones, show that hunting and fishing were common in Ubaid times.

An aerial view of Tarut village taken c.1950. The ruined fort, possibly of Portuguese origin in the 1520s, sits atop a mound formed by successive layers of occupation reaching back to the third millennium BC. The palm-frond dwellings (*barastis*) in the foreground, are built using a similarly ancient method of construction and are still common today.

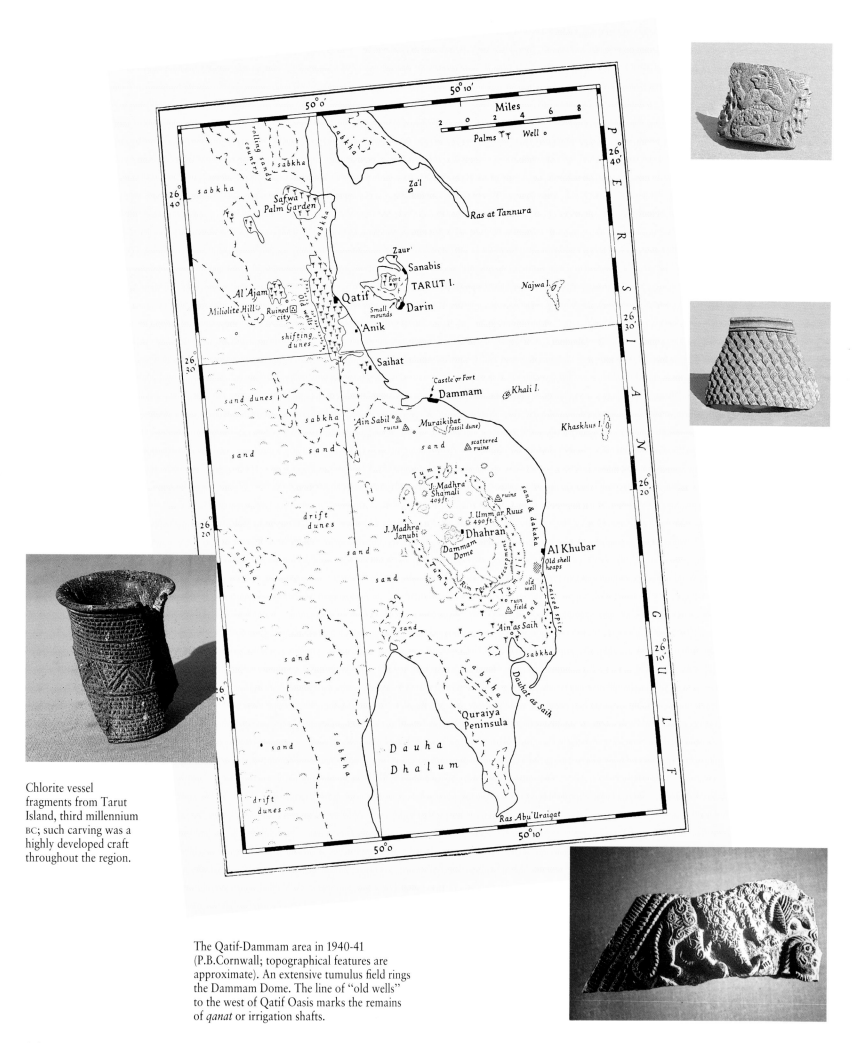

Chlorite vessel fragments from Tarut Island, third millennium BC; such carving was a highly developed craft throughout the region.

The Qatif-Dammam area in 1940-41 (P.B.Cornwall; topographical features are approximate). An extensive tumulus field rings the Dammam Dome. The line of "old wells" to the west of Qatif Oasis marks the remains of *qanat* or irrigation shafts.

A pot of Barbar type from Bahrain, third millennium BC, found on Tarut.

supported by the discovery in Hasa Oasis of what is thought to be third millennium pottery on low mounds adjoining drainage channels and near wells and springs.

Hasa Oasis is the largest and most obvious candidate for large-scale settlement in the whole of eastern Arabia, although for this – as for later periods – archaeological evidence in the area is curiously elusive. In the United Arab Emirates and Oman, however, evidence is plentiful, and it sheds much light on the development of early oasis agriculture.

Meanwhile, rock art from central and northern Arabia shows the indigenous people of Arabia gradually evolving during the Neolithic period from hunters and gatherers to herdsmen of sheep, goats and cattle. The domestication of the camel was yet to come. These people inhabited the Syrian Desert and the northern, central and eastern parts of the Peninsula. They used rough seasonal structures – surviving today as stone circles – and long elaborate V-shaped structures, known as "kites", for trapping game. Parts of their domains were of course contiguous to Mesopotamia. The Sumerians, who spoke a non-Semitic language with no known relatives or descendants, and their Semitic-speaking successors the Akkadians, knew this race as the *MAR-TU* or Amorites: a rough, tent-dwelling, herding people. Many *MAR-TU* names are recorded and these show, first, that the *MAR-TU* were Semitic-speakers, and second, that Mesopotamian society increasingly had to absorb *MAR-TU* groups throughout the third millennium BC and after. Evidence of *MAR-TU* names on Dilmun, such as the tribe of Agarum, suggests that its population, at least from the third millennium but possibly from the earliest times in the Ubaid period, can be seen as a mixture of the indigenous Arabian pastoralist or Amorite people with Ubaid and Sumerian elements.

Where archaeological evidence of the living is lacking on the mainland, evidence of the dead more than compensates. The inhabitants of eastern Arabia and Bahrain, like their contemporaries in the United Arab Emirates and Oman, developed a taste for funerary tumuli which seems to have outlasted the Dilmun culture and continued right down to the early centuries AD. Most spectacularly, Bahrain's

tumuli are estimated to number some 170,000. But a vast tumulus field also ringed the Dammam Dome on the mainland. Of some 50,000 or more estimated to have been there in the 1940s, less than 2,000 have survived the subsequent development of the area. Of those remaining only a small number have been investigated, and the evidence suggests that they cover several different periods of use, with many being re-used in later periods. Many date from the first millennium BC; but a significant number belong to the third millennium BC. Like the finds from Tarut Island, some pre-date the tumuli on Bahrain, corroborating the view that we should look to the mainland of the Eastern Province for Dilmun's original location.

Further inland, near Abqaiq, complexes of tumuli stand on ridgelines overlooking a large Neolithic lake and an extinct drainage channel which passed from Hasa Oasis to the Gulf.

The significance of Dilmun to Gulf civilisation was both mythical and worldly. Its sanctity was associated in the Sumerian mind with the origins of their own civilisation and with the pursuit of immortality. One of their major gods, Enki, who lived in the Apsu, or Abyss, was the god of the sweet waters under the earth. This is itself a telling concept, for in al-Hasa and Bahrain fresh water from underground aquifers wells up in abundance both on dry land and under the sea. It is quite

A large storage jar from an Abqaiq tomb, c.2500 BC.

A Dilmun-type pot found on Tarut, third millennium BC.

27

possible that the Sumerians believed that al-Hasa and Bahrain derived their sanctity from this association.

The famous Sumerian epic of Gilgamesh tells the story of the hero-king of that name who, in pursuit of the flower of eternal youth, comes to Dilmun and is directed to plunge into the sea (perhaps one of the maritime freshwater springs) where he finds the flower. Gilgamesh, however, is robbed of eternity by a serpent who devours the bloom and the king returns to his city resigned to his mortality.

Other legends have identified Dilmun with the story of the Garden of Eden; but evidence for all such claims purporting to verify the myth, tends to be tenuous.

Dilmun's worldly role was as a vital trading centre and entrepôt for goods from further down the Gulf. Dilmun's merchants handled a wide range of goods, converting, for example, copper ore into ingots for shipment to the Sumerian cities,

which lacked raw materials of their own. Dilmun ships also brought fine stone, such as diorite, which was carved into statues of the gods and kings. Dilmun's own exports included dates, onions, cloth and what perhaps were pearls or beads, described in the ancient texts as "fish-eyes". Dilmun's

The reed boat, *Tigris*, built by and sailed under the direction of Thor Heyerdahl to demonstrate the long-distance capabilities of third millennium reed vessels.

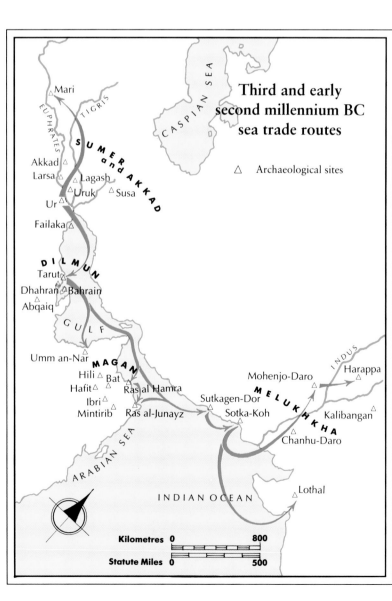

Third and early second millennium BC sea trade routes

△ Archaeological sites

merchants had their own distinctive types of stamp seal, with which the ownership of goods could be marked and documents authenticated. And there also appears to have been a standard Dilmunite system of weights and measures, though it has been suggested that this was identical with the one used by the Indus Valley cities. Real personalities emerge from the Mesopotamian records, such as Ea-Nasir, a member of the guild of Dilmun merchants, who lived c.1800 BC.

Water transport was of particular importance to these early societies, as it is thought that the camel had not yet been domesticated as a beast of burden. Evidence from seal impressions suggests that the first trading vessels were probably made of reed bundles lashed together. The effectiveness of this method of boat-building was demonstrated by Thor Heyer-

dahl's reconstruction the "*Tigris*", in which he sailed round Arabia from the Gulf to the Red Sea.

Oasis farmers and camel nomads

With instability in Mesopotamia and the disruption of trade in the Gulf after c.1700 BC, the character of mainland eastern Arabia's archaeology changes. There is a gap in the archaeological record in the Eastern Province, as in most of Saudi Arabia, for much of the second millennium BC. Brilliantly crafted trade goods seem to disappear; we are left with remains which are hard to date in a cultural context, and hard to interpret.

Profound changes were certainly taking place in Arabia. By the late second and early first millennia BC, trading settlements were springing up on overland routes from the Yemen, and long-distance trade had been transformed by the use of the domesticated camel as a beast of burden.

Maybe part of the answer lies in climatic change. Towards the end of the third millennium the climate became drier. This made life more difficult for the herders and hunters of central and eastern Arabia. Many would have become more dependent on the oases and wadis by taking up the agriculture which was already being practised in them. At the other extreme some groups of hunters and herders would have had to increase their mobility to exploit diminishing natural resources.

Agriculture certainly already involved the date palm, a native of eastern Arabia and southern Iraq. Other crops included barley, wheat and sorghum, all three of which have been discovered in archaeological deposits dating to the mid-third millennium BC in the United Arab Emirates. Agriculture in these areas would have depended, as today, upon irrigation, and crops are best raised in the partial shade within or adjacent to palm groves. During the third millennium the abundant natural waters of Hasa Oasis, Qatif, Tarut Island and the northern part of Bahrain Island would have provided ideal conditions for these early oasis farmers.

What of those groups which were forced to increase their mobility? Originally sheep and goat herders, they were no

more mobile than donkeys would permit, and were therefore relatively powerless compared to their camel-borne successors. The evidence suggests that the camel was first domesticated as a milk animal somewhere in southern Arabia during the third millennium BC. Camels appear on a tomb of Umm an-Nar type in the United Arab Emirates, dating to the mid-third millennium. This does not prove that the camel was domesticated, but its importance to the owner of the tomb suggests so. As it became drier, so camel pastoralism spread.

The nomadic life of camel herding, characteristic of life in Arabia for at least the last 3,000 years, is a highly specialised existence. It would have taken centuries to evolve. The initial use of the camel as a milk animal probably augmented the herding of sheep and goats, and it may

A family on the move in the Eastern Province, c.1950. The nomadic way of life traces its origins in eastern and southern Arabia to the second and third millennia BC.

have taken time before its uses as a beast of burden were realised. Subsequently its capabilities as a riding animal and its use in battle were developed. So there emerged throughout Arabia specialised nomadic camel-breeders, reliant upon the camel. They used vast ranges of land, and learned to exploit the military potential of the beast in large numbers. We do not hear of large-scale use of the camel as a beast of burden until the end of the second millennium. Camel-riding Arab tribesmen in battle first appear even later in the historical record – in the ninth century BC.

The descendants of the Amorite pastoralists were transformed, in the second millennium, into economically and militarily powerful tribes: oasis farmers and traders at one extreme, specialised camel pastoralists at the other. These groups were the ancestors of the Arab tribes.

One record of the highly centralised third millennium settlements declining during the second millennium is provided by the Kassite governor of Dilmun, writing in c.1370 BC. He sent a vivid report of conditions there: a nomadic people whom he calls the *Akhlamu* had plundered all the dates and pillaged the settlements. Elsewhere, in Mesopotamia, the *Akhlamu* have been identified with the Aramaean nomads, who emerged as a political force in the previously Amorite areas. (Possibly they were the same people under another name.) The episode illustrates a new feature of life in Arabia: nomads could pose a military threat to settlements and carry off plunder in large quantities. Both suggest that the *Akhlamu* were camel nomads, though their mode of transport is not specified.

In the ninth to seventh centuries BC, Assyrian records of campaigns in northern Arabia show that tribally organised *Arubu* (i.e. Arabs) occupied the deserts and oases of northern and northwestern Arabia. They were capable of putting large numbers of camel-riding warriors into the field, and were engaged in the trade with south-west Arabia. By the sixth century BC, caravan towns such as Tayma and Dedan in the north-west were well-established. From then on, nomads and settlers were to become interdependent not only for resources, but also for the operation of the lucrative overland trade. The Eastern Province and its people were to continue to be at the junction of influences from central and south-west Arabia, the Aramaean sphere, and from southern Iraq.

CHAPTER THREE

The Age of Overland Trade

Caravan routes and markets

IN ANTIQUITY, Arabia's overland routes and seaways along the Gulf and Red Sea provided the commercial link between the worlds of the Mediterranean and Indian Ocean. Trade began in earnest at least as early as 500 BC. After the conquests of Alexander the Great (d.323 BC), his Seleucid successors took control of Syria and Mesopotamia. Greek traders and goods became familiar in eastern Arabia at this time, which seems to mark the initial period of prosperity in this part of the Peninsula.

The trade reached a peak during the early centuries of the Roman Empire (30 BC – c.AD 200), when vast quantities of luxury goods, largely spices and aromatics, were transported from the Yemen, East Africa, India and China to satisfy the enormous demand in the Roman world. The frankincense and myrrh of ancient Yemen were prized commodities in this trade, and the merchants of the Sayhad cultures of the Yemen played a vital role in the passage of goods from the Indian Ocean onto the land routes of Arabia.

The goods were carried by camel caravan via Najran, up western Arabia to the Mediterranean. This was probably the most ancient route, in operation at least by Assyrian times in the eighth century BC. A succession of states grew up to control the trade at the northern end, of which the most celebrated were the Nabataeans (third century BC – AD 106), who built Petra as their capital.

By the fourth century BC, another route had evolved. This ran from Najran to Qaryat al-Faw and Wadi Dawasir, and then skirted the northern side of the Empty Quarter, crossing southern Najd via Aflaj and Kharj. Its destination was the great trading centre of eastern Arabia, Gerrha, which controlled the onward shipment of goods to Iraq, both overland and by sea. Gerrha also controlled whatever trade was sent overland from the Gulf to north-west Arabia and the eastern Mediterranean.

This pattern of trade was of course affected at different periods by the relative ascendancy of the Gulf and Red Sea as trade routes, by political conditions along the land routes, and by developments in maritime technology.

For example, some time around 100 BC Greek sailors in the Red Sea discovered how to use the south-west monsoon winds, enabling them to sail directly from Egypt to India and back again with their cargoes, by-passing the Yemen. The more fragile indigenous stitched vessels of the Indian Ocean were unable to withstand the strong winds of the south-west monsoon season, from May to September, and so were laid up in port. Direct sailing would have adversely affected the amount of trade that was carried overland. Nonetheless, the total volume of trade seems to have been sufficient to sustain the overland routes. Later, the Romans continued to encourage direct sailing, but it was the economic slump in the Roman Empire in the third century AD which dealt a blow to the

An incense burner from Thaj.

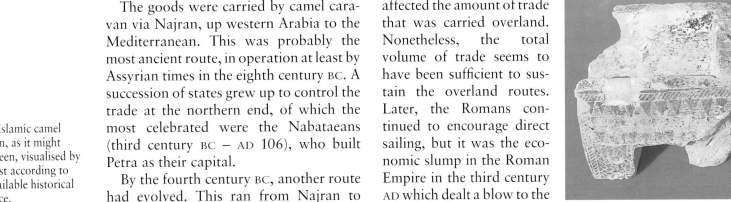

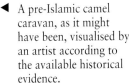

A pre-Islamic camel caravan, as it might have been, visualised by an artist according to the available historical evidence.

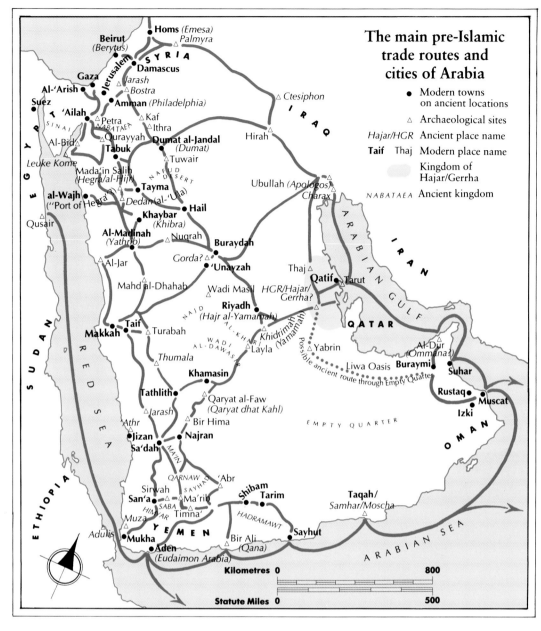

The main pre-Islamic trade routes and cities of Arabia

- ● Modern towns on ancient locations
- △ Archaeological sites
- *Hajar/HGR* Ancient place name
- **Taif** Thaj Modern place name
- ▨ Kingdom of Hajar/Gerrha
- *NABATAEA* Ancient kingdom

thians supported a governor or vassal ruler there in the early third century.

A new stimulus appeared in the Gulf with the Sasanids (AD 225-636), a Persian dynasty which replaced the Parthians. They established their capital in Mesopotamia at Ctesiphon, later to be known by the early Muslim conquerors as Mada'in. Sasanian policy was to control not only the Gulf but the trade of the Indian Ocean too, and to strangle the Red Sea as a rival artery of commerce. In implementing this policy they brought the Eastern Province into their sphere of influence. By AD 570, they had actually succeeded in taking control of the Yemen by means of an invasion by sea. Much of their effort in Arabia was aimed at countering Byzantine influence during the centuries before Islam, and during this time the trade routes became arteries not only of trade but of political and cultural influence.

The lost city of Gerrha

Due to the growth of the overland trade, the early part of the first millennium BC saw a revival of settlement in the Eastern Province. Assyrian records refer to Dilmun during the period c.750-600 BC, and the final mention is a Neo-Babylonian one during the reign of Nabonidus in the mid-sixth century BC. Some of the excavated Dhahran tumuli have yielded finds of this time, such as stamp and cylinder seals which show trade contacts with Egypt, Iraq, Syria and the Yemen, as well as pottery, steatite vessels, incense burners, and one of the typical Neo-Babylonian "bathtub" clay sarcophagi.

The city-state of Gerrha dominated life in the Eastern Province between c.700 BC and the early centuries AD, thriving on the vigorous revival of commercial interest in the region. It is quite possible that the remains from the Dhahran tumuli could well have been left behind by Gerrhaean traders. The city's existence is confirmed by the writings of contemporary geographers and historians and also by the discovery of ancient coins. However, the precise location remains a mystery. The sparse finds of several archaeological sites contend for the right to be known as the lost city of Gerrha.

This gravestone from Tarut Island, late first millennium BC, records, in Greek, the passing of a local notable: Abeibil Nouma, Farewell (*ABEIBHΛ NOYMA XAIPE*).

prosperity of land and sea routes alike.

In the Gulf, the Parthians of Persia (c.140 BC – AD 225) controlled the maritime trade to Mesopotamia. They had a less ambitious maritime policy than their Sasanian successors, but learned to extend the range of direct sailing, making it unnecessary to stop at ports in eastern Arabia. Probably as a result, overland trade from the Gulf to the Mediterranean shifted northwards in the first century AD from the Gerrha-al-Qasim-Taima route to one via Charax and Palmyra. Despite the slump in the aromatics trade after AD 200 (as a result of reduced demand in the Mediterranean), the settlements of the Eastern Province remained important as communication links between the Yemen on the one hand and the Gulf and Iraq on the other. It is almost certain that the Par-

Early Accounts of Gerrha.

After sailing along the coast of Arabia for a distance of two thousand four hundred stadia, one comes to Gerrha, a city situated on a deep gulf; it is inhabited by Chaldaeans, exiles from Babylon; the soil contains salt and the people live in houses made of salt; and since flakes of salt continually scale off, owing to the scorching heat of the rays of the sun, and fall away, the people frequently spray the houses with water and thus keep the walls firm. The city is two hundred stadia distant from the sea; and the Gerrhaeans traffic by land, for the most part, in the Arabian merchandise and aromatics, though Aristoboulos says, on the contrary, that the Gerrhaeans import most of their cargoes on rafts to Babylonia, and thence sail up the Euphrates with them, and then convey them by land to all parts of the country.

Gerrha period copper tools with iron fittings, from Tarut.

STRABO (23 BC) *Geography* 16.3.3, quoting Eratosthenes, 3rd century BC.

The Gerrhaeans begged the king [Antiochus] not to abolish the gifts the gods had bestowed on them, perpetual peace and freedom. . . . When their freedom had been established, the Gerrhaeans passed a decree honouring Antiochus with the gift of 500 talents of silver, 1000 talents of frankincense, and 200 talents of stacte [myrrh].

POLYBIUS (208-176 BC), *Histories* 13.9, recording the campaign of Antiochus III, Seleucid ruler of Syria, in c.205 BC. The Gerrhaeans were wealthy enough to buy Antiochus off.

The Bay of Gerrha and the town of that name, which measures five miles around and has towers made of squared blocks of salt. Fifty miles inland is the Attene district; and opposite to it and the same number of miles distant from the coast is the island of Tyros [meaning Tylos, Bahrain] extremely famous for its numerous pearls.

PLINY, *Natural History* 6.32.147, quoting from a report prepared for Ptolemy Epiphanes (205-181 BC).

An alabaster bowl from Tarut.

From their trading both the Sabaeans and the Gerrhaeans have become richest of all; and they have a vast equipment of gold and silver articles, such as couches and tripods and bowls, together with drinking vessels and very costly houses; for doors and walls and ceilings are variegated with ivory and gold and silver and set with precious stones.

STRABO *Geography* 16.4.19.

Strabo (c.64 BC – post AD 21), the Greek geographer, suggests that Gerrha was founded in about the sixth or seventh century BC and this would accord with the finds at Dhahran. Among those sites that have been proposed for Gerrha are Thaj, Qatif, Dhahran, 'Ayn Jawan near Safwa, 'Uqayr and the "Salt Mine Site" north of 'Uqayr. This latter, near the extensive *sabkha*s north of 'Uqayr, on the coast, has yielded a few finds of the same period, and the site itself appears to be part of a large, ancient field system, located at the mouth of an ancient "river" which drained Hasa Oasis.

The most convincing arguments suggest that Gerrha lay somewhere in Hasa Oasis, with its huge natural springs. It is hard to deny that it must have been the population and food production centre of the region, and therefore the political and commercial centre. It was certainly so in the late pre-Islamic, Early Islamic and succeeding periods. Moreover, land routes from the Yemen, Najd and Iraq naturally converge upon the oasis. If the name Gerrha is derived from the South Arabian *HGR* (*Hajar*) and Aramaic *Hagara*, as seems to be the case, then the name of Hajar for the capital of the Oasis in late pre-Islamic and Early Islamic times would seem to clinch the identification.

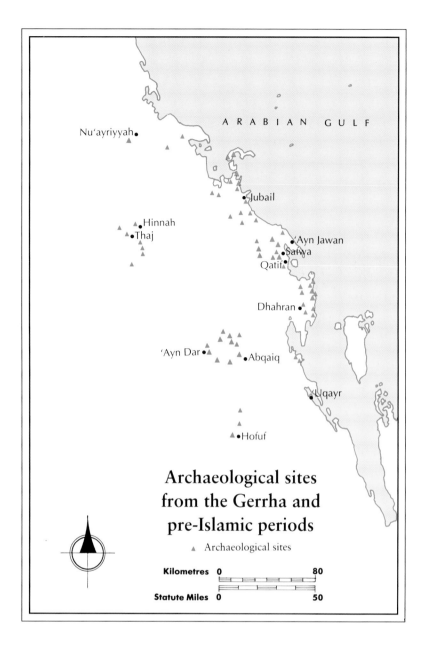

Archaeological sites from the Gerrha and pre-Islamic periods

▲ Archaeological sites

Kilometres 0   80

Statute Miles 0   50

liyyah, is the site of ancient Gerrha because of the supposed similarity of the name. Others have claimed that the name of Gerrha is echoed today in that of the Jabal Qarah district of the Oasis. Neither contention is supported by archaeological evidence, nor are these two place-names in fact close to Gerrha etymologically, whereas Gerrha/*Hagara*/*HGR*/Hajar equate very satisfactorily.

Whether Gerrha lay on the coast or inland is another issue yet to be resolved. The likelihood is that it lay inland and was served by a "port of Gerrha" on the coast – a configuration which has parallels elsewhere on the arid coast of Arabia. 'Uqayr fulfilled this function in recent times for Hasa Oasis; similarly, Jubail may have done so for Thaj.

If, as seems to have been the case, the flow of water through the oasis was greater than that of recent times, extensive areas north-east of the present-day oasis could have been cultivable. Indeed, Hasa Oasis appears to have been shrinking steadily from the north-east since at least early Islamic times, accounting for the present isolation of important Early Islamic sites such as Jawatha. We can therefore imagine that cultivation during the Gerrha period was much more extensive than recently, supporting a thriving population with a highly developed oasis agriculture. The date palm, cereals, and some fruit and vegetables (though not today's wide range) would all have been grown. The famous white donkeys of Hasa may

Fragment of a votive clay figurine from Thaj.

The problem is that no major city site of this period, particularly not one which would fit the connotation of *HGR* meaning a walled city with gates and towers, has yet been found in Hasa Oasis. Indeed, surprisingly few finds at all from this period have come to light there. This may be because both Hasa and Qatif Oases, unlike other site areas, have been continuously inhabited and farmed ever since, obliterating much, especially buildings of sun-dried mud. There are two large, apparently pre-Islamic occupation areas outside the northern plantation areas of Hasa Oasis, near Mubarraz and Jawatha, which may repay examination. Still others may await more detailed investigation.

Some have claimed that a locality named Jar'a, on a slight elevation near the edge of the cultivated area between Mubarraz and the historic village of Batta-

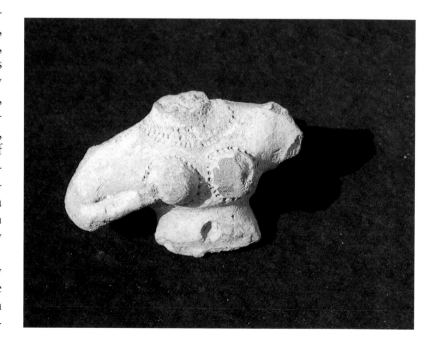

Fragments of camel figurines from Thaj.

already have been providing the power for irrigation and load-carrying. We know little as yet of crafts and industries, for which Hasa Oasis was later to become renowned. But it seems certain that, in material terms, the major features of oasis life, which it retained until lately, were either developing or already in place.

North of Hasa Oasis, the heavy concentration of sites in the 'Ayn Dar/Abqaiq area suggests that there was a major settlement there, as yet undiscovered. It may have been inundated by the sands, encroaching fast in recent centuries.

Further north still, the ancient trade route would have brought the caravans to Thaj. This is the only known site in the Eastern Province whose remains fit the meaning of *HGR*. Furthermore, Thaj is the only site in the region at which coins of the Kings of *HGR* have been found. And the geographical evidence for the location of Gerrha given by the Greek and Roman geographers can be made to fit Thaj as well as Hasa Oasis. In contrast to Hasa Oasis, Thaj has not been extensively inhabited since pre-Islamic times. This, and the use of stone in construction, have ensured that much survives to be seen today.

Thaj is one of the largest archaeological sites in the Kingdom. Several seasons of excavations by the Saudi Arabian Department of Antiquities, starting in the early 1980s, have revealed that even if it was not Gerrha, it was a town of exceptional size and prosperity. It lay on a major route from Hasa to southern Iraq, and another ancient route (known in recent times as the Darb al-Kunhuri) may have crossed it, running from Jubail to the Riyadh area, ancient Hajr al-Yamamah, via the Dahna'

sands and Rumah Wells.

The limited excavations so far have revealed that the site was probably first occupied in the late fourth century BC, and was inhabited until the fourth century AD, while the abundant pottery suggests that the city flourished from c.300 BC until the first century AD. The total length of the city wall, which was over four metres thick with towers at the corners, is over two and a half kilometres. Today its entire length can be seen clearly only from the air. The wall was built of ashlar masonry with rubble infill, perhaps in the third century BC. Settlement was concentrated within the walls, though there are also extensive remains outside. The *sabkha* to the north of the site may have had a shallow lake at the time. If so, the local water table would have been higher in antiquity. More probably, however, the *sabkha* we see today is the result of a long period of run-off irrigation water draining from the ancient fields, and it may have been the increasing salination of the soil which eventually made the area uninhabitable on a large scale. There are many large ancient stone-lined wells, testifying to the agricultural activity of the time.

Finds from Thaj include numerous so-called Hasaean inscriptions in the local pre-Islamic dialect (using an essentially Sabaean script), several Aramaic inscriptions, silver and copper coins, pottery, and figurines of people and animals, particularly camels.

It is thought that the three *jabal*s to the east of Thaj may have been sacred "high places". Five kilometres to the north-east is the small town site of Hinna, which is contemporary with Thaj. Earlier this century Hinna was a settlement of the Ikhwan, the brotherhood of reformist bedouin settlers fostered by Ibn Saud, who used the ancient masonry to build their own settlement, itself now also in ruins.

Wherever Gerrha is to be located, its ports and heavily populated coast, particularly in the Safwa and Qatif areas, were important points on the Gulf sea route, while Hasa Oasis, Thaj and the 'Ayn Dar/Abqaiq area were major points on the land route. The period is marked by vigorous agricultural exploitation of areas barren today, which were, at the same time, located on or near the major communication and trade routes.

Fragments of clay figurine from Thaj.

The names of some of the settlements of the state ruled by the Gerrhaeans are known from the Greek geographer Ptolemy, who compiled his data in c.AD 150. According to Ptolemy, Gerrha was situated on the coast. His information illustrates two points: the possibility that Gerrha still existed in the second century AD, and that the Gerrhaeans presided not over an isolated trading centre, but a substantial portion of eastern Arabia from Thaj in the north to perhaps Qatar in the south – a situation which was to be repeated in Early Islamic times when the province of eastern Arabia, then known as al-Bahrain, was ruled from Hajar in Hasa Oasis.

The Gerrha period represents, after the Dilmun period, the second climax of prosperity in the history of the Eastern Province. Its commercial importance through the centuries is reflected in the many influences discernible in its archaeological finds: Assyrian, Neo-Babylonian, even Egyptian; then Greek, Aramaic, Nabataean, and Roman. In addition, Parthian influence has been detected in jewellery found at the Jawan Tomb near Safwa, and contacts with India can be deduced from a statue, now lost, originally discovered in Qatif Oasis.

As a whole, the period spanning the 800 years to c.AD 270 is characterised, in tribal Arabia, by the ascendancy of prosperous settled cultures. The riches derived from overland trade, despite being tribally based, seem to have stimulated the development of centralised states, combining both commercial and military power.

At the zenith of this process was the Nabataean kingdom with its capital Petra which was finally annexed by Rome in AD 106. Also highly developed was the state of Palmyra whose armies swept through the eastern provinces of Rome in the 270s. As far as is known, Gerrha was chiefly a commercial force. It is possible that, as evidence comes to light, Gerrha may come to be recognised as a third example of pre-Islamic Arab statehood.

Sasanid Persia and the pre-Islamic Arab tribes

The third century AD saw an economic slump in the Mediterranean world. This, coupled with a much diminished demand for incense after the Roman adoption of Christianity in the fourth century, brought decline to the Yemen and the caravan towns along the Arabian trade routes. The end of commercial prosperity wrought adjustments in Arabian society during the four centuries until the dawn of Islam.

For as long as the trans-Arabian trade

The abandoned village of Hinna near Thaj c.1950. Established by the Ikhwan in the early twentieth century, the village made use of large stone-lined wells of the Thaj period.

from the Yemen continued, the settlements of the Eastern Province would have played a role in it. However, income from trade must have been much reduced after the first century AD as the sea trade of the Gulf began to by-pass the Eastern Province. Trading cities like Thaj and Gerrha would have lost their former wealth, and with it their dominance. Nonetheless, agricultural settlement in the great oases of al-Hasa and Qatif must have continued to flourish, markets for local products would still have been necessary, and coastal settlements dependent on fishing and pearling would have survived.

The economic decline of the towns co-incided with the growth of the nomadic way of life. A series of tribal migrations took place from south-west Arabia into central, eastern and northern Arabia. This was to dramatically change the tribal face of the Eastern Province. Settlements re-

---

Language and scripts in pre-Islamic eastern Arabia

Some of the historical evidence for this period comes in the form of pre-Islamic inscriptions. The chief script in use during the Gerrha period was the same as the Sabaean script of pre-Islamic Yemen. It was used to write the Hasaean language, which, from the meagre evidence available, appears to have been a dialect closely related to the other pre-Islamic dialects of Saudi Arabia.

Most of the known Hasaean inscriptions come from Thaj. Others are from Hinna, Qatif, Ras Tannurah, Abqaiq, 'Ayn Jawan, and Uruk in southern Iraq. Nearly all the Hasaean inscriptions are gravestones, giving information as to names and tribal relationships. Aramaic and Greek inscriptions also occur in the Eastern Province.

A Hasaean inscription (Ja 1044) from Qatif Oasis: "Memorial and tomb of Lahayhawn, son of Hawn'abd, son of 'Afnay, he of the clan Sa'ad'ay."

---

mained important as food producers and markets; some also took on status as neutral places where hostilities were suspended so that influential local families might settle disputes. But political power in Arabia came increasingly to be held by tribal warrior aristocracies.

As one would expect, little archaeological evidence survives from a society such as this, although excavation of a camel burial in one of the Dhahran tumuli throws some light on funerary practices.

In fact, the evidence for the history of this period is drawn not so much from archaeology as from documentary and literary sources: inscriptions, Byzantine writers, early Muslim historians, Arab tribal traditions, and the pre-Islamic poets whose work, oral in origin, was written down in early Islamic times. The origin of today's tribes and clans in eastern Arabia can be traced to the pattern of those days.

After AD 300, perhaps because of the loss of economic power, the Arabs in the north on the frontier between the Roman and Persian empires became increasingly dominated by their imperial neighbours. Rome's successor, Byzantium, absorbed a series of warrior clans at the head of tribal confederations into the Byzantine system of defence against the Persians in Mesopotamia. This was done by paying subsidies and conferring status on their leaders.

In opposing the Romans and Byzantines, the Persians pursued a similar policy: they set up the Arab Lakhmid clan as a buffer state. The Sasanians maintained the Lakhmids as client lords of a powerful tribal confederation with their capital at Hirah, where the deserts of north-eastern Arabia border the Euphrates alluvium. From here the Lakhmids intervened continually in the affairs of the tribes of eastern Arabia for most of the centuries preceding Islam. For their part, the Sasanians could choose whether to engage directly in the affairs of the Eastern Province, or to exercise indirect influence from the Iraqi marches through their Lakhmid clients.

In the south, there was a third centre of power: the Himyarite kingdom of the Yemen, which in c.AD 300 united the previously fragmented city states of southwest Arabia. Like the Persians, the Himyarite rulers pursued a policy of setting up and supporting a powerful tribal confederation in central Arabia as a means of exerting influence. In the fifth century AD this tribal confederation, Kinda, became sufficiently powerful to pursue its own interests in central Arabia. By the early sixth century it actually succeeded in taking over the Lakhmid capital Hirah. From ancient al-Yamamah (the area of Kharj and Riyadh today) and Hirah, the Kindites controlled the Eastern Province for a short time, though by AD 528 the Sasanians had managed to restore the Lakhmids.

This map, published in Holland in 1611, is an early example of a map based on the coordinates of the Greek geographer Ptolemy, who compiled his data c.AD 150. Ptolemy places Gerrha on the coast. The other main towns named in his manuscripts as within the area of Gerrha's influence are Magindanata, Bilbana, Sata, Domana, Atta, Sarcoa, Catara, Ibirtha, Masthala and Phigeia, which was probably Thaj.

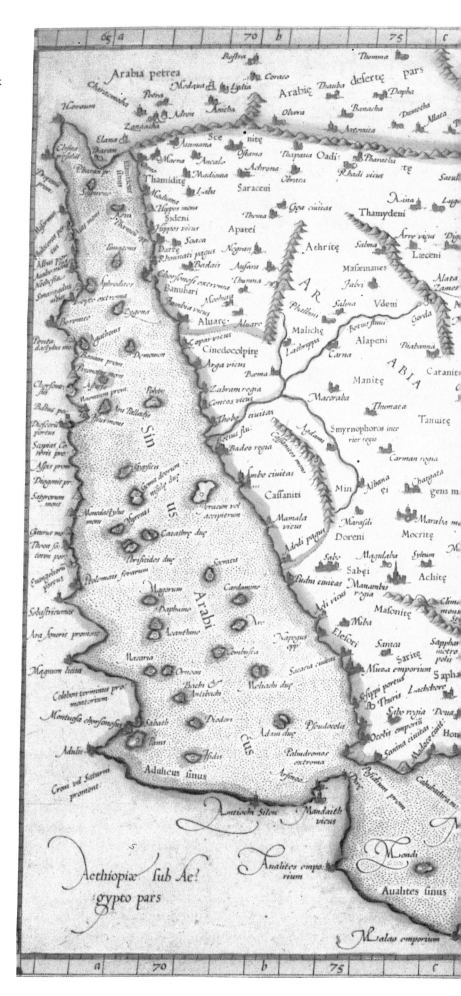

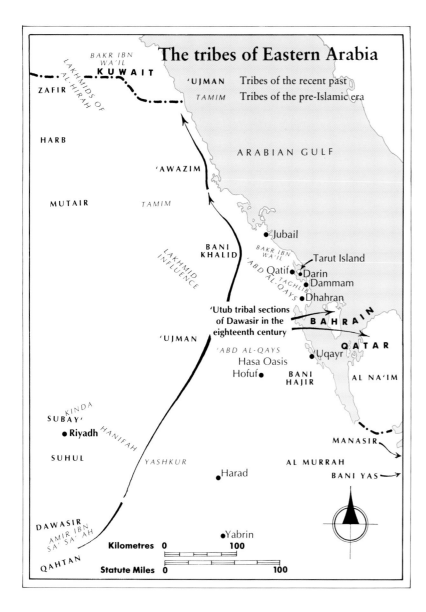

The Sasanians exercised a profound influence on the Eastern Province. In AD 225 they replaced the Parthian dynasty in Persia, and immediately began to pursue a vigorous policy of expansion in the Gulf. Their King Ardashir invaded the Eastern Province in AD 228, ousting the Parthian governor and appointing a Sasanian one in his place. Ardashir also founded a new city, Batn Ardashir or Pit-Ardashir, on the site of the former city of Khatt. Its location has so far eluded archaeologists, but most scholars agree on its most probable identification: somewhere in Qatif Oasis.

In the early fourth century AD, apparently because of a drought that was afflicting their lands, Arab tribes from the Hasa area raided the Persian coast. The Sasanian King Shapur II responded in about AD 325: in a series of campaigns he attacked the Tamim, Bakr ibn Wa'il and 'Abd al-Qays, the chief tribes of the Eastern Province. He then marched on al-Yamamah in Najd, and from there crossed the Peninsula to Yathrib (later al-Madinah), turning north to threaten the Roman frontier of the Provincia Arabia. He is credited with all kinds of brutality, including piercing the shoulders of prisoners so that they could be bound together – from which he was dubbed "Dhu al-Aktaf", or "Lord of the Shoulders". Members of the 'Abd al-Qays and Tamim were re-settled at Hajar in Hasa Oasis, some of the Taghlib and Bakr were settled at Darin on Tarut Island and at Khatt, while other groups were deported to Persia.

Sasanian policy in Arabia was essentially anti-Roman and anti-Byzantine, and Shapur's expedition has to be seen in the light of this. Indeed, much of the history of the tribes and towns has to be seen in terms of factions supporting Persia or Rome/Byzantium.

Fundamentally it was a question of commerce: the Sasanians had been remarkably successful in establishing control of both sides of the Gulf and, in doing so, creating a monopoly of trade from the Indian Ocean, plied via the Gulf to Iraq. In order to counter this, the Byzantines aimed to develop once more the Red Sea route to India. To this end, they entered into relations with trading communities along the western land route of Arabia such as Makkah and Najran, campaigned in the Red Sea, and allied themselves with the rulers of Ethiopia, where Christianity had taken root. Inevitably, the Yemen became a region of conflict between the two rival powers, and the Sasanians endeavoured to bring their influence to bear there, by entering into relations with the tribes who controlled the land route through the Eastern Province and southern Najd via Kharj and Wadi Dawasir.

The other major development of the period was religious. Arabian society, in common with the rest of the contemporary civilised world of the Mediterranean and the Middle East, was profoundly drawn by the new religious currents towards monotheism. By the sixth century, Christianity, Judaism, Zoroastrianism, and even an Arabian religion centring on a single deity named Rahman, had all made inroads into the paganism prevalent at the time. Monophysite and Nestorian Christianity in particular found converts in Arabia. Religious currents tended to reflect the political allegiance of their sources, and, hence, the Byzantines supported Monophysite communities while the Sasanians supported the Nestorians who, from c.AD 400, established bishoprics at Darin, Qatif, Hajar and on Muharraq Island off Bahrain.

The Arab tribes who were by now well established in the Eastern Province were the 'Abd al-Qays, with their centres at Hajar and Jawatha in Hasa Oasis, Bakr ibn Wa'il, Tamim and Taghlib, all of whom counted Christians among their number. The 'Abd al-Qays were the chief settled tribe, while the other three were mainly nomadic, although they too had settled sections. A sub-tribe of 'Abd al-Qays, Jadhima ibn 'Awf, was based in Qatif Oasis in a centre named Zara, which later also served as the base for a Persian garrison. Zara's location has never been identified – possibly its remains lie beneath the sands encroaching on the western edge of the oasis area. Another branch of 'Abd al-Qays inhabited Dhahran, and it is likely that the oasis area of Qatif in those days covered the entire coastal stretch between Safwa in the north and Dammam and Dhahran in the south. As in later times, the major oasis settlements would have had a large number of non-tribal people in them too, especially those on the coast where foreigners were resident.

Shortly before the dawn of Islam, the Sasanians appear to have opted for direct rule of the Eastern Province by installing a governor at Hajar in Hasa Oasis. This perhaps reflected their need to keep close control over their Arabian allies during their occupation of the Yemen, which they had invaded by sea and taken in AD 570. The governor occupied a fortress known to the Arabs as Mushaqqar, which was situated on a great water channel called Muhallim. Hence we can see that at this period the Oasis was clearly farmed on a large scale. Also at Qatif Oasis, the impressive remains of an underground *qanat* system of drainage shafts just outside the western edge of the palms, points to Persian influence in farming and irrigation, and so perhaps date to the foundation of Pit-Ardashir or later in the Sasanian period. This line of *qanat*s, now being engulfed by the sands, also suggests that the cultivated area of Qatif Oasis extended further inland at that time than it does today.

Princes and poets

In about AD 500 the rule of the Lakhmids of Hirah was broken by the Kinda, an independent tribal confederation at the height of its power. For about thirty years the Eastern Province came under Kindite rule – a period which was remembered as a kind of golden age of tribal independence. By AD 531 Kindite power had collapsed, and the Lakhmids had been restored.

Pre-Islamic poets and Arab historians preserve further reports illustrating the tribes' relations with the Sasanians and among themselves after AD 600. The poets occupy a special position in pre-Islamic Arabia. They might either be noble themselves or they would attach themselves to a powerful patron. Their eloquence as satirists and propagandists was a potent political instrument in desert affairs. Their work, though oral in origin, was passed from generation to generation until it was written down in Islamic times, and forms an important source for pre-Islamic Arabian history. The tales are written in classical Arabic and concentrate on heroic themes: honour and shame, both personal and tribal, prevail over morality and guilt. The tribal virtues of loyalty, courage and generosity are extolled and the pleasures of life acknowledged. Man is depicted as locked in solitary struggle against fate. A sense of the transience and ultimate pathos of human existence pervades these works.

One story of plunder and revenge tells of a caravan of gifts sent by Wahriz, the Persian ruler of Yemen, to the Sasanian King Chosroes II. As they approached al-Hasa the caravan was ambushed by a group of Tamim who butchered most of the envoys and guards and carried off the Persian gifts. The survivors of the caravan fled to Hawdha ibn Ali, chief of the Hanifah in al-Yamamah and an ally of the Persians; under his protection the men were brought safely before Chosroes in Iraq. Hawdha was rewarded and crowned by Chosroes who then sent him back to Hasa Oasis with orders to punish the Tamim. The latter had assembled at the fortress of the Persian governor at Hajar to obtain food after the harvest. On the pretext of distributing grain, the governor invited them into the fortress of Mushaqqar. Once inside, the factions responsible for the raid on the caravan were coolly massacred. Hawdha arrived in time to intercede in favour of some of them, but the vengeful slaughter became known as "The Day of the Barred Gates of Mushaqqar".

Laments after battle: Seventh Century poetry

O rider, if thou lightest on those men who drank with me
  in Najran aforetime, say – "Ye never shall meet him more!"
Abu-Karib and those twain al-Ayham my boon-fellows,
  and Qays of al-Yaman there in the uplands of Hadramawt.
May God pay their meed of shame to Madhhij for al-Kulab
  - the noble of blood that fell like rabble the sons of slaves!
  Had it been my will, my mare was ready to fly with me
  - behind her the black steeds lag, and slacken, and drop away:
But it was my will to stand and fight for your father's house,
  and his doom of old is known who stands as his fellow's shield.

> PART OF THE DEATH-SONG of 'Abd-Yaghuth, chief of the Banu 'l-Harith of Najran, after their defeat by Tamim at the second Battle of Kulab between al-Yamamah and the Dahna' Sands, AD 612 (Tr. Lyall)

My comrade rebuked my grief as we passed by a place of graves,
  and down from mine eyes fell fast a burden of streaming tears:
He said – "Dost thou weep each grave thou seest because of one
  that lies in the waste twixt ad-Dakakik and al-Liwa?"
I answered him – "Nay: pain wakes from slumber the pain of old;
  so let me alone: all these to me are but Malik's grave."

> THE POET MUTAMMIM, on his grief at the death of his brother Malik, chief of the Yarbu' clan of Tamim, during the war of the *riddah* or Apostasy, c.AD 633. (Tr. Lyall)

The dawn of Islam

In a political sense, the four centuries following the third century AD marked a low point in the fortunes of the Arabs of central and eastern Arabia. Hemmed in by the great powers of the day, and deprived of the rich commercial opportunities which had brought prosperity to Gerrha, they had reverted to tribal factionalism which was exploited by the Sasanians, Byzantines and Himyarites.

In the early seventh century, eastern Arabia was still in a state of tribal unrest in an uneasy relationship with Persian rule of the settled areas. When the call to embrace Islam came in c.627-9, the settlements of Hasa Oasis were ruled jointly by an Arab, Mundir ibn Sawa, a Christian thought to be of the 'Abd al-Qays, and a Persian governor in Mushaqqar/Hajar. Mundir was quick to adopt the new faith, and a delegation was sent to the Prophet in

Madinah to conclude a treaty. It is said that the first taxes, in the form of dates and grain, received by the Muslim government, came from the Eastern Province.

Islam offered an alternative not only to Persian rule, but also to the old tribal rivalries, by proposing allegiance to a larger ideal. This was to transform, in an astonishingly short time, the fortunes of the Arabs of the Peninsula. By introducing a new ideal of man's relationship with the One God, and with it a new ideology of state and society which taught the equality and brotherhood of all Muslims, it was to inspire the Arabs and take them to the far corners of the civilised world.

45

CHAPTER FOUR

Since the Dawn of Islam

The early centuries

DUE to the early conversion of the 'Abd al-Qays tribe, Islam was quick to take root in the Eastern Province. Jawatha, their town in Hasa Oasis, boasted the first mosque in Arabia outside Madinah: its carefully preserved remains can still be seen, although the town of Jawatha is little more than a name today. In the 620s, during the lifetime of the Prophet, Islam made steady progress and contacts with the Islamic government and teachings in Madinah were strong.

While inland al-Hasa was controlled by the Arab tribes, the coast was still nominally governed by the Sasanians. After the Prophet's death in 632, some of the tribes rebelled against the new Islamic state, so playing a part in the wars of the *riddah*, or Apostasy, which rent Arabia from 632 to 634. Not for the last time, the threat to al-Hasa came from the north, in the form of a coalition of the Bakr ibn Wa'il and the former rulers of Hirah. Marching on Hasa Oasis, they laid siege to Jawatha.

However, the Prophet's successor Abu Bakr despatched al-'Ala ibn al-Hadrami to relieve the 'Abd al-Qays who had remained loyal to Islam. The siege was lifted and the besiegers dispersed. The 'Abd al-Qays, under al-'Ala, and their famous leader Jarud, marched on the coast, penning the Persians into their stronghold in Zara in Qatif Oasis, and converting Tarut Island and the other coastal communities.

Eastern Arabia now began to look outwards. The 'Abd al-Qays led seaborne expeditions against the Persian coast, and

participated in the final conquest of Fars in 649-50. From around this time the entire Arabian seaboard of the Gulf as far as Oman came to be incorporated into a single province under the great new Muslim foundation of Basra. Basra in the early days had become a great military centre, drawing in many of the tribesmen of the Eastern Province, particularly of 'Abd al-Qays, Bakr ibn Wa'il and Tamim, all of whom took part in the Muslim conquest of Persia and Khurasan.

As Islam spread into the Indian Ocean, al-Hasa contributed ships and men to the expeditions. Despite the maritime orientation of expansion, coast and hinterland were united under the tribal Arabs of the interior in the outward thrust of conquest: for example, the leader of the Hasawi expedition to India in the 660s was from Hajar, once again chief town of Hasa Oasis. One of the fruits of this expedition was an elephant, a gift for the Umayyad Caliph Mu'awiya based in Damascus.

During the Umayyad period (661-750) the Islamic state, then a single entity extending from North Africa to Iraq and Iran, was ruled from Damascus. The Umayyad Caliphs after Mu'awiya were faced by various groups which questioned Umayyad ideology and went under the name of "Kharijites", or "those who go out". One of the most prominent leaders was Najdah ibn 'Amr al-

An Eastern Province tribesman, c.1950.

In the Governor's palace, Hofuf c.1950.

The preserved section of the mosque at Jawatha, Hasa Oasis, held to be the first mosque in Arabia outside al-Madinah.

Hanafi, of the district around Riyadh and Kharj which was known as al-Yamamah. He and his followers subdued the 'Abd al-Qays of al-Hasa, and for a few years exerted control over much of the Arabian Peninsula. The Umayyads reasserted control from Basra in 692, restoring the 'Abd al-Qays, and consolidating Hajar as a stronghold. But, for the remainder of their rule, the Umayyads had to endure intermittent uprisings in al-Hasa.

The Abbasid assumption of power in 750, and the removal of the Islamic capital to Baghdad, ushered in a new golden age of trade in the Gulf which was to last until the tenth century. As before, eastern Arabia with al-Yamamah had a series of governors appointed from Baghdad. What little resistance there was to the Abbasids was led by the 'Abd al-Qays, but Hajar remained as the chief town and administrative centre. The Gulf ports and merchants involved in the trade to India and China grew immensely rich; Siraf in particular, on the Persian side, flourished, but Arabs played an increasing role in the trade, as witnessed by the rise of Suhar in Oman, and the stories which grew up around Arab traders such as Sulayman the Merchant, Abu Zayd Hasan of Siraf, and Abu Ubaydah of Suhar. It was the stories woven around the lives of the merchants, sailors and rulers of this period which gave rise to the tales of Sindbad the Sailor.

The port of Hasa Oasis, 'Uqayr, is mentioned in the 840s as a port of call for Basra, Oman, China and Yemen, and a large archaeological site there probably dates to this Early Islamic period. The importance of eastern Arabia to the Abbasid treasury is confirmed by the very large revenue collected from there – greater than Oman, and almost as much as the Yemen.

The Qarmatians of al-Hasa

In the latter part of the ninth century Abbasid control began to disintegrate, and the Islamic world was riven by various dissident movements, many of them of Ismaili inspiration. One of these movements, originating in Iraq, took root in eastern Arabia. Known as the Qarmatians, after their first leader Hasan Qarmat, they took Qatif in 899, burned Zara and went on to capture Hajar. They then set about establishing a tightly organised state under the Qarmatian missionary Abu Sa'id al-Jannabi, with its capital at the city of al-Hasa, their new foundation either on the site of or just outside the old city of Hajar in the Oasis. With coast and hinterland closely united, and with the help of tribes who had recently moved into the Eastern Province from southern Najd, they extended their rule and influence into Iran and southern Iraq.

The Qarmatian period marks a climax in the political history of Hasa Oasis, even if, ideologically, the movement was heterodox and has even been seen by some scholars as standing altogether outside Islam. In their first and most militant phase, from 886 till 935, the Qarmatians raided Basra, Kufah and Wasit frequently, and disrupted the pilgrimage. In 930 they committed the ultimate sacrilege, assaulting Makkah and taking the Black Stone from the Ka'bah back to al-Hasa. In 931 Abu Sa'id's son, Abu Tahir, handed over government to a Persian Magian, only to realise his mistake after eighty days of turmoil during which various outrages and abominations were committed. This episode marked a turning-point in the Qarmatians' religious extremism.

The second phase, 935-988, saw a rapprochement with the Abbasid state, during which the Qarmatians assisted Baghdad in repelling Fatimid expansion from Egypt into Syria. The Black Stone was returned to Makkah, and Qarmatian doctrine seems to have returned to a more orthodox Islamic form. Cooperation with the Abbasids was directed also against the rising Buyid dynasty of western Iran. In 983 the Qarmatians invaded southern Iraq but, in 988, they were defeated by the Buyids and their bases in al-Hasa and Qatif were plundered.

The early Islamic geographer Muqaddasi, writing in the 980s, refers to the Qarmatian domain as both al-Hasa and Hajar. Their city, he says, was the capital of the Qarmatian dynasty of Abu Sa'id, which ruled the province of Hajar, also known as al-Bahrain. It was surrounded by palm groves, and was prosperous and densely populated. A day's march from the sea, it was the commercial centre of the entire region. Government was watchful and fair, but the great mosque was abandoned and there were no prayers. Yaqut, writing in the thirteenth century, adds that the city of al-Hasa was surrounded by a wall built by Abu Tahir in 929.

The Qarmatians resumed control of eastern Arabia after the setback of 988, but the last period of their rule, 988-1073, was marked by a lessening in their power and prosperity, due in part to the rise of Egypt and the Red Sea trade from the Indian Ocean at the expense of that through the Gulf. It is from this phase that we have an eye-witness account of al-Hasa, from the Ismaili propagandist Nasir-i-Khusraw, who travelled through southern Najd and eastern Arabia in 1051.

'Uyunids and 'Usfurids at Qatif

Qarmatian decline in al-Hasa accompanied the rise of the Saljuq Turks to the north. During the eleventh century they progressively established their rule over Iran, Iraq and northern Syria. In 1073 an 'Abd al-Qays leader from 'Uyun, in the north of Hasa Oasis, overthrew the Qarmatians with Saljuq help and established a dynasty, the 'Uyunids, which ruled until 1253.

The first 'Uyunid ruler, Abdullah ibn Ali, took over the city of al-Hasa as his capital. However, the decline of al-Hasa as a regional power, and its consequent isolation from the main political currents to the north, led to an increasing focus on the coast. Although times were less prosperous in the Gulf, trade was still lucrative, and the 'Uyunid rulers were drawn into rivalry with the chief centre of Gulf power in these centuries, the Arab merchant rulers of Qays Island off the Persian coast.

The name Lahsa designates at once a town, a district, a suburb and a stronghold. Four strong concentric walls, solidly built in mud and about a parasang* apart from each other, surround the town. Lahsa contains abundant springs, each of which is sufficient to turn five mills, and all the water is so well utilised that none of it flows outside the walls. A beautiful town rises in the centre of the fortified enclosure. It contains everything which goes to make a great city, and there are more than twenty thousand inhabitants ready to carry arms. Formerly its ruler was a leader who led the people outside the way of Islam. He exempted them from the obligations of prayer and fasting . . . The descendants of Abu Sa'id live today in an enormous palace which is the seat of government. There is in this palace a dais on which these six personages take their place to pronounce, having reached agreement among themselves, their orders and decrees. They are assisted by six vizirs who sit behind them on another dais. All business is decided by them in council. When I was in Lahsa, these princes owned thirty thousand black slaves, bought with silver, who were employed in agriculture and gardening. The people paid no taxes or tithes. If anybody fell into poverty or debt, he was given loans until his affairs recovered. If anyone contracted a debt, his creditor reclaimed only the capital. Every foreigner with a trade received, on arrival, a sum of money available to him until he had ensured his means of support . . . There are mills at Lahsa which are the property of the state in which grain is milled into flour for private citizens without charge. The maintenance of these mills and the pay of the workers is met by the government . . . Currency for transactions is in the form of lead contained in baskets . . . They manufacture in Lahsa high-quality waist-cloths which they export to Basra and other places . . . In the sea of Bahrain there is pearl-fishing; half of the pearls collected by the divers belong to the chiefs of Lahsa . . . Dates are so abundant in Lahsa that they give them to their animals as feed.

The communal character of Qarmatian rule emerges clearly from this account. Indeed, to this day a characteristic feature of Hasawi culture has been the absence of the notion of the private ownership of the large water sources. The centralised government and agricultural development under the Qarmatians described by Nasir-i-Khusraw is confirmed by the archaeological record, which shows that large areas in the northern part of the Oasis were under cultivation, for example that around Jawatha.

---

* 1 parasang = approximately 5 kilometres

Throughout the twelfth century, fleets from Qays raided Bahrain Island and Qatif. The latter had become the seat of 'Uyunid government, and Hasa Oasis was ruled from it. Qatif replaced 'Uqayr as the port of the Eastern Province; Bahrain Island, then known as Uwal, was also controlled by the 'Uyunids who, by the end of the twelfth century, were forced to share the taxes of the coastal domains with the Qaysi rulers.

By the thirteenth century Qaysi dominance began to be threatened by a new maritime power, Hormuz, at the mouth of the Gulf. The 'Usfurid rulers of al-Hasa, who replaced the 'Uyunids in 1253, now allied themselves with Qays in fending off the challenge from Hormuz. In doing so they brought prosperity to the Eastern Province: by the early fourteenth century its dates, pearls and especially horses were in great demand in the international trade to India.

In the 1330s Qays finally yielded its control of the Gulf trade to Hormuz. But the Eastern Province seems to have been little affected by the change. Though the Hormuzis made some effort to establish

their rule over Bahrain Island and Qatif, there is no evidence to suggest that their control was effective. The 'Usfurids maintained their independence, ruling from Qatif, and life in al-Hasa generally seems to have continued at a reasonably prosperous level. The great north African Arab traveller Ibn Battutah visited both Qatif and Hajar ("now called al-Hasa", he says) in the 1330s, noting in particular that Qatif was a large, prosperous and beautiful city. Concerning Qarmatian doctrines he records not a trace. In al-Hasa he was astonished by the vast palm groves, and quotes the well-worn proverb, "like carrying dates to al-Hasa", the Arab equivalent of the English "carrying coals to Newcastle".

During the following century trading conditions continued to improve, and by 1400 the Gulf was entering upon a new age of prosperous commerce. Goods from India and China once again poured through into Iraq, and the island of Hormuz reached its zenith as a trading power, becoming legendary in the West. In 1440 the 'Usfurids ceded power to a new tribal dynasty, the Jabrids.

The Jabrids, the Portuguese and the Ottoman Turks

The Jabrids originated in the desert around Hasa Oasis. First taking the town of al-Hasa, they made it their seat of government, and then set about extending their control to the coastline. They quickly transcended their desert origins, becoming settled amirs with a reputation for just rule, and renowned for their piety and attention to the rulings of the 'ulama, the religious advisers whose opinions formed the basis of Islamic government.

Jabri power extended to Bahrain Island, south to Oman, and westwards to Kharj in southern Najd. Their first and most noted ruler, Ajwad ibn Zamil al-Jabri, sent great pilgrimages across Arabia: the largest in 1507 was some 30,000 strong. The earliest extant building still in use in Hofuf dates from the Jabri period: the Jabri Mosque, near Qasr Ibrahim.

Strong central rule, favourable environmental conditions in eastern Arabia, and the continuing increase in Gulf trade, combined to bring prosperity to an indepen-

Inside the Jabri mosque, Hofuf.

drawn on to the wider stage of international conflict, as efforts were made from Iraq to counter the Portuguese during the sixteenth century.

Establishing bases in East Africa, southern Arabia and India, the Portuguese also, in 1515, captured Hormuz. In concert with the Iranian Safavid dynasty, they took Bahrain and, in 1520, sacked Qatif, killing the Jabri ruler Muqrin, who had refused to pay tribute to Hormuz. Terminally weakened, the Jabrid state fell prey in 1524 to the ruler of Basra, Rashid ibn Mughamis.

Al-Hasa and Bahrain were in fact caught in a tripartite international struggle: the rising power of Ottoman Turkey, intent on extending its empire into Iraq and protecting its commercial interests from the Portuguese, the newly emergent Safavid dynasty of Iran which saw itself as the regional rival of the Ottomans, and the Portuguese who were often brutal in pursuit of their commercial aims.

Between 1534 and 1546 the Ottomans took over Basra, and from there and Suez on the Red Sea they organised the maritime fleets to oppose the Portuguese and patrol the Gulf. In 1549 they moved on al-Hasa, occupying Qatif first and then moving inland. Forts were built at 'Uqayr and Qatif to protect the trade. But they failed to dislodge the Portuguese either from Bahrain, formerly part of the Jabrid domain, from Hormuz, or from Muscat.

The Ottomans chose Hofuf, known to them as Lahsa, as the capital of the new province. Qasr Ibrahim was used as the barracks and administrative centre, and the great Mosque of Ibrahim there dates to this period. A battalion of Janissaries, the

dent al-Hasa. But international developments were soon to bring profound changes. In 1498 the Portuguese rounded the Cape of Good Hope and, in so doing, were to alter completely the pattern of Indian Ocean trade. They set about creating a maritime empire by force of arms, the aim of which was to divert the rich trade from India and the Far East to Europe round the Cape, away from the Gulf and Red Sea. They were remarkably successful, and the Islamic states which had hitherto controlled the trade, as well as the Venetians in the eastern Mediterranean, suffered accordingly. Al-Hasa had been

The fort at Tarut (c.1950), thought to have been built by the Portuguese in the 1520s.

The Ottomans made concerted efforts to thwart Portuguese ambitions in the Gulf. This Portuguese manuscript of 1564 shows the Ottoman fleet (*right*) assembled at Cape Musandam in 1554 to confront the Portuguese fleet at Muscat (*left*).

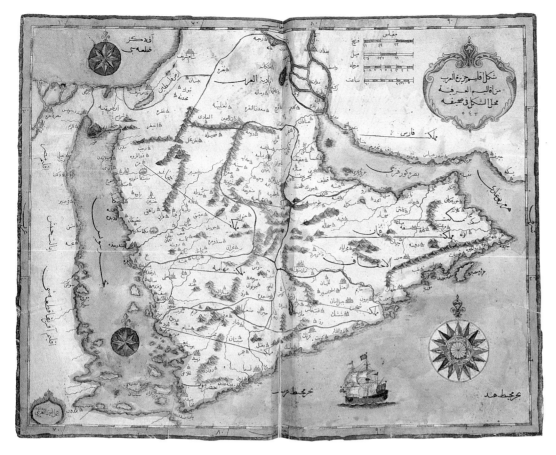

An Ottoman map compiled after the Ottomans had relinquished their hold on al-Hasa, printed in Istanbul, 1732. Lahsa, Qatif and Bahrain are named.

in the Portuguese interest to block Gulf trade, and the Ottomans profited from the trade routes at the head of the Gulf.

By 1600 the Portuguese threat was fading. The conduct of trade by force of arms began to give way to the "era of the companies", in which English, Dutch and French associations of merchants, such as the English East India Company, sought to do business with local rulers by agreement rather than coercion. In 1622 the English and Persians expelled the Portuguese from Hormuz. Though the Portuguese continued to trade in the Gulf – they are on record as buying pearls and the finest Arabian horses from the shaykh of Qatif, which they sold in India – their days were numbered. Between 1630 and 1700 Gulf trade was dominated by the Dutch. Thereafter the English East India Company was to establish its supremacy.

However, Ottoman energies were also flagging. After 1600 their hold on al-Hasa weakened, largely due to a lack of money, making way for the re-emergence of local rulers. After 1620, when the Persians captured Basra, the province was severed from direct financial support from Istanbul. Ottoman government continued to operate at a reduced level until 1680, when the Al Humayd, a clan of the Bani Khalid tribe, expelled the remnants of the garrison.

Sultan's élite troops, was stationed in the province – some 800 men, augmented by up to 300 local militiamen. Firearms were introduced, necessitating the improvement of fortifications. A full land registration was organised as a basis for levying taxes, and customs revenues were systematised. Nomadic shaykhs were enrolled as salaried officers in order to bring order to the desert, as far south as Yabrin and north to Kuwait. The Ottoman system of Shari'ah law and court records were introduced. The Ottoman archives shed a light on the details of life in al-Hasa – its bureaucracy, land ownership, military, economic and judicial organisation – which is unrivalled from any previous period.

Though by the final years of the sixteenth century the Ottomans had failed to wrest control of the trade of the Gulf and Red Sea from the Portuguese, they had succeeded in consolidating control of al-Hasa. Their income from the Hormuz customs meant that it was not entirely

The Mosque of Ibrahim, Hofuf, built by the Ottomans in the sixteenth century.

A seventeenth century graffito of an Ottoman janissary in Qasr Ibrahim, Hofuf.

Bani Khalid rule and the First Saudi State

The Bani Khalid tribe were a powerful force in eastern Arabia, controlling the entire desert region from Basra in the north to Qatar in the south. The tribe consisted of both nomadic and settled groups. Al Humayd restored local, traditional tribal rule to al-Hasa. They set up their centre of government just outside Hofuf, at Mubarraz, today the second town of the Oasis but in those days probably little more than a stopping place for caravans and an area for tribal encampment. The demands of government created a need for more permanent facilities, as was the way with other takeovers of Arabian towns by nomadic tribes, and Qasr Sahud, the great fort of Mubarraz, probably dates to this time.

Hasa Oasis remained a powerful local force, but under the Bani Khalid its interests became divorced from those of the coast. During the seventeenth century the 'Utub, a group of clans from southern Najd, migrated into eastern Arabia and established a client relationship with the Bani Khalid. By the early eighteenth century they were in Kuwait, and their transformation into successful maritime traders had begun. In 1766 they founded Zubarah on the Qatar coast, and in 1782 they took control of Bahrain. It is from these 'Utbi clans that today's ruling families of Kuwait and Bahrain are descended.

Meanwhile, Hasa Oasis maintained a landward orientation. During the eighteenth century the Bani Khalid played an important role in the affairs of central

The nineteenth century Ottoman barracks in Qasr Ibrahim, Hofuf.

The ruined fort at Dammam (1934), possibly the one which served as a base for the notorious Rahmah ibn Jabir until 1826.

Arabia, protecting the growing regional power there of 'Uyaynah, and attempting after 1745 to impede the rise of the Reform Movement and the House of Saud at Dir'iyyah, 'Uyaynah's great rival. The Reform Movement was the purified form of Islam advocated by Muhammad ibn 'Abd al-Wahhab. However, the Bani Khalid failed to curb the militant progress of the Movement and, in a battle at Ghuraymil south of Qatif Oasis in 1790, themselves fell victim to it.

So came the Eastern Province's incorporation into the First Saudi State. Fortifications in Hofuf were repaired and extended.

The Ottoman government's response to these events was made in al-Hasa. An expedition led by the Muntafiq chief, Thuwayni, ended with his assassination, before he even reached Hasa Oasis. The second attempt, in 1799, was better organised. Capturing Hofuf, it set about dislodging the remaining Saudi garrison in Qasr Sahud at Mubarraz.

The defence of Qasr Sahud deserves a prominent place among the many feats of heroism and endurance for which the tribal Arabian warrior has been justly renowned. The besiegers numbered some ten to twelve thousand men, the defenders no more than one hundred. Yet they resisted — for almost five months — a continuous assault which drew upon virtually every technique of siege warfare: artillery, bombardment from wooden towers, and mining beneath the walls. Thoroughly demoralised, the besiegers abandoned their occupation of the Oasis in despair and withdrew to Iraq.

Al-Hasa served as the Saudi State's outlet to the sea, by which it made its first contact with international concerns, notably the East India Company and consequently the British. The British were intent on securing the passage to India via the Gulf. This involved suppression of Arab freebooters, intensive marine surveys, and — as a general policy — the cultivation of good relations with the Ottomans.

Al-Hasa, together with Zubayr near Basra, was also the gateway through which imported goods, chiefly textiles and firearms, made an increasing appearance in eastern and central Arabia.

The Second Saudi State

In 1818, the First Saudi State fell to an Egyptian/Ottoman invasion force, led from the Hijaz by Ibrahim Pasha, which captured Dir'iyyah after a long siege and subsequently destroyed it. The Egyptians moved into Hasa Oasis and Qatif, and seem to have toyed with the idea of occupying Najd and the Eastern Province. However, as it soon became clear that the resources of the country were inadequate to maintain an occupation, and the insecurity of communications too great, they decided in 1819 to evacuate. Al-Hasa reverted to Al Humayd rule.

The British were now seeking to ensure the security of the Arabian side of the Gulf. Hence, British visitors were beginning to make their appearance in al-Hasa: Sadleir in 1819, Wyburd in 1832, and Jopp in 1841. From Sadleir's report it is clear that Qatif had declined in commercial importance as an entry point for goods into the Eastern Province. Its place had been taken by Bahrain, and 'Uqayr was merely of local importance in its role as the port of Hasa Oasis.

In 1824 the Saudi Imam, Turki ibn Abdullah, revived Saudi fortunes, choosing Riyadh as the capital of the Second Saudi State.

Stability returned with the Imam Faisal's escape from exile in 1843 and the re-establishment of his rule. There followed twenty-two years during which the Saudi State enjoyed comparative peace, though within less extensive borders than those of the First. The Imam's reign was marked by a new circumspection in dealings with foreign powers, particularly the Ottomans and the British. He was able to consolidate the achievements of the Reform Movement in administration and order in the desert and the settlements. Economically, peace brought a measure of prosperity to al-Hasa. Date and cloth exports increased, as did the trade in horses, which was flourishing elsewhere at this time in Najd.

Once again, al-Hasa formed the Saudi state's chief access to the sea, and imports, amongst which manufactured goods were becoming increasingly common, flowed through it from Bahrain. In 1861 the British, by formalising the Perpetual Treaty of Peace in the Gulf, took over responsibility for Bahrain's foreign relations. This had the effect of ending hostilities between Bahrain and al-Hasa.

As before, the Saudis, supported by the men of al-Hasa, attempted to influence events in the southern Gulf and Oman by garrisoning Buraymi, but its freedom of action was limited by Britain's increasing involvement with the rulers of the region.

In 1862 Hasa Oasis was visited by the British traveller Palgrave, who had traversed Arabia from Syria via Hail, Buraydah and Riyadh. A somewhat inaccurate observer of his surroundings, his veracity has been doubted by some. There can be no doubt, however, that he actually visited the oasis. In his vivid account of Hofuf and Hasa Oasis, where he was warmly received, he describes the Kut, Rifa'ah and Na'athil quarters, the market, the mosque, the architectural style and the weavers, metal-workers and other artisans: a busy, cosmopolitan town of, he thinks, some 24,000 people (his population estimates are notoriously unreliable) under a Saudi governor headquartered in the Kut.

Palgrave proceeded to Qatif, also under a Saudi governor, and took ship for Bahrain. Three years later he was followed by Pelly, the British Political Resident in the Gulf, but Pelly did not stay long enough to take detailed note of his surroundings. He had come on official business to see the Imam Faisal in Riyadh. Shortly after his visit, in 1865, the old, blind Imam died.

Qasr Sahud, Mubarraz, today.

Renewed Ottoman occupation, 1871-1913

The Ottomans were to rule al-Hasa until 1913. Headquartered at Hofuf, they immediately set about modernising its administration. Al-Hasa was made a *sanjak*, or district, curiously named by the Ottomans the "Sanjak of Najd", of the province of Basra. By the 1880s Qatar had been added as a sub-district of the new *sanjak*. The other two subdistricts were the capital itself with Hasa Oasis, and Qatif. Bahrain remained firmly under British protection.

A Provincial Administrative Council was set up which included local representatives, as did government at the sub-district level. Judicial reforms reflected those elsewhere in the Ottoman Empire: the standard Ottoman codification of Islamic law was introduced, judges were appointed from Istanbul, and an appeals procedure instituted. A police force maintained law and order. Schools and a military hospital served the Ottoman community. Port facilities were improved at Qatif and 'Uqayr, guard towers built and customs offices set up. A Municipality building was erected in Hofuf. It was, on the face of it, a satisfactory state of affairs for the people of al-Hasa, but the evidence suggests that financial difficulties in the Empire at large meant that the *sanjak* was on balance drained of revenue, and hence that investment was kept at a bare minimum. Also the Ottomans, unlike their Saudi successors after 1913, failed to impose law and order on the desert tribes,

The Suq al-Khamis, Hofuf, in 1905, during Ottoman rule.

with the consequence that trade and communications suffered greatly.

The occupying garrison was drawn from the Ottoman Sixth Army Corps based in Baghdad. By 1893 the total had risen to 424, most of whom were quartered in Qasr Ibrahim, which was re-developed as a barracks and administrative complex.

In 1874 'Abd al-Rahman ibn Faisal, the brother of Saud and the Imam Abdullah, tried to take Hofuf from the Ottomans. Landing at 'Uqayr, he rallied the 'Ujman and Al Murrah to his cause, took Qasr Khuzam at Hofuf, and laid siege to the garrison in Qasr Ibrahim. But he was defeated by a relief force of Ottoman troops and Muntafiq tribesmen at Waziyyah, between Mubarraz and 'Uyun.

Hofuf was then plundered by the Muntafiq, and many leading Hasawi families fled to Bahrain.

Apart from this episode, Ottoman rule spared the Eastern Province any further involvement in the decline of the Second Saudi State which was to result, in 1891, in the ascendancy of Hail over central Arabia and the departure of 'Abd al-Rahman, now head of Al Saud, into exile in Kuwait. Al-Hasa was disturbed only by local diffi-culties, notably with the desert tribes – for example a confrontation between the 'Ujman and the townsfolk of Mubarraz and Kilabiyyah in 1906. Such problems were resolved by local mediation. On one occasion, in 1909, the Ottoman governor was assassinated as a result of a dispute with the people of Mubarraz.

The Saudi recovery of al-Hasa

In January 1902, in a daring dawn raid on the Masmak Fortress in Riyadh, the young son of 'Abd al-Rahman ibn Faisal Al Saud, 'Abd al-'Aziz, with a force of only forty men, seized control of Riyadh. It was the beginning of a new chapter in the history of Saudi Arabia: betweeen then and 1932 the future King 'Abd al-'Aziz was to unite the regions of Arabia which today comprise the Kingdom.

By 1911 he had consolidated much of central Arabia, including al-Qasim and southern Najd, under Riyadh's hegemony. Having already confronted the Ottomans in al-Qasim, he was concerned that further expansion would bring him up against the interests of outside powers.

He was also deeply aware, like his grandfather the Imam Faisal, of the inherent instability of the tribal scene. He sought, with the religious leaders of Riyadh, to counteract this by an initiative

Ibn Saud's force on campaign near Thaj, March 1911.

north of Sudayr. This was soon followed by many others. By 1917 there were over 200 of them, many of them in the Eastern Province. They represented a community of zealous believers, whose men were in a state of constant readiness for action. Increasingly, they became the backbone of Ibn Saud's forces in his campaigns to unify the Kingdom.

By 1913 'Abd al-'Aziz was in a position to threaten the Ottoman occupation of al-Hasa. Descending by forced marches on the oasis in May, he entered Hofuf by night and mounted a nocturnal assault on Qasr Ibrahim. The garrison was taken by surprise and speedily capitulated. The Ottoman troops were allowed to evacuate via 'Uqayr, and Qatif surrendered soon after. A few Iraqi Ottoman officials stayed on to assist the new government, but the Eastern Province had been returned to Saudi rule.

To begin with, however, Ibn Saud's control of al-Hasa was by no means certain. The 'Ujman tribe, whose opposition to Saudi rule dated back to 1845, even beyond its support of the Imam Abdullah's brother and rival Saud, refused to lay down its arms. In 1915 they ambushed a Saudi force at Kinzan, between Kilabiyyah and Jawatha, killing about three hundred Hasawis as well as Ibn Saud's brother Sa'd. They followed this up by plundering the oasis towns and villages.

1915 marked a low point in 'Abd al-'Aziz's fortunes. In January he had tried to neutralise the threat from Hail in the north at the indecisive battle of Jarrab;

of visionary boldness: to replace divisive tribal loyalties with a larger loyalty to creed and state. Its implementation involved settling the bedouin, teaching them agriculture and inculcating into them the tenets of Islamic reform. Settlement would render them accessible to the beneficial effects of religious instruction, education and commerce.

The first settlement appeared in an astonishingly short space of time, at the wells of 'Artawiyyah in Mutayr territory

Ibn Saud (*seated, centre*) and his entourage at Thaj, March 1911. His brother Sa'd stands to his right.

Sa'd, the brother of Ibn Saud, killed at Kinzan in 1915.

and Captain Shakespear's death there had robbed him, just after the outbreak of the First World War, of an important influence on British policy. In the west, Sharif Husayn had for several years been exerting pressure on his territories from the Ottoman-dominated Hijaz, and was coming to be seen by the British as a more effective ally against the Turks, with whom they were then at war. Nonetheless, Ibn Saud managed rapidly to retrieve the situation in al-Hasa, calling up reinforcements from Riyadh and harrying the 'Ujman out of the oasis. The flight of the 'Ujman northwards towards Kuwait signalled the end of tribal troubles in the Eastern Province.

The Province settled down and, once again the Saudi state's window on the outside world, experienced a measure of prosperity. Government was entrusted to Ibn Saud's respected cousin Abdullah ibn Jiluwi. Security brought prosperity, and imports flowed in. A new building in Hofuf, the arcaded Qaysariyyah market, was added to the eastern side of the Suq al-Khamis. A fine royal palace rose near Qasr Ibrahim.

Until the incorporation of the Hijaz into the Saudi state in 1925, 'Abd al-'Aziz's contacts with the outside world were conducted through the Eastern Province. Important negotiations with the British took place at 'Uqayr – in 1916-17 and 1920-22 – at first to clarify Britain's support for

The main door of the Gosaibi house, Hofuf, in 1937 (*left*). Built in the early 1920s next to the Qaysariyyah Market, its elaborate plaster decoration is Gulf-influenced.

Riyadh in its conduct of the war (against the Ottoman Turks) in the Middle East, and later to establish the line of the frontiers with Iraq and Kuwait.

By 1926 the form of the Kingdom had been established: both northern Arabia and the Hijaz had been incorporated, and the Eastern Province had become part of a much larger entity. Frontiers with Transjordan, Iraq and Kuwait had been formalised. The first diplomatic missions were received, not in al-Hasa, but in Jiddah. Riyadh's meagre revenues had been somewhat boosted by pilgrimage receipts. Modernisation was in the air, with the first introduction of wireless telegraphy, motor cars and the rudiments of a delegated administration. By 1932 the Saudi borders had assumed almost the shape which they have retained to the present day, and the young state was proclaimed the Kingdom of Saudi Arabia.

The newly formed Kingdom was in fact about to take a far greater leap into the future than anyone can have imagined. If the Eastern Province's importance to the emergent state had been diminished by the acquisition of a Red Sea coastline, the eclipse was only temporary. For, in 1938, oil was discovered beneath the Dammam Dome in commercial quantities. During the following decades, the wealth of the Eastern Province was to attract, not for the first time in its history, the eyes of the world.

Ibn Saud and Sir Percy Cox at the 'Uqayr conference, 1922. Standing behind them is Major Frank Holmes, who was granted the first concession to search for oil in al-Hasa.

61

CHAPTER FIVE

The People

Nomad and settler in the Eastern Province

SEEING life in the Eastern Province today, transformed as it has been in little more than a generation, it is often difficult to discern the background from which it has so recently emerged. This background continues to be a formative influence on the character of the region and its people.

The key to an understanding of Arabia lies in acknowledging the sparseness of its resources and the precariousness of existence. Its people, tribal and non-tribal, followed a variety of ways of life, from the truly nomadic to the semi-nomadic and settled. Across this range of adaptations, an entire society tried to maximise the use of the slender resources available. Thus, if disaster struck, another option was available: settled people might adopt the nomadic life, and vice versa.

The nomads and semi-nomads herded of camels, goats and sheep, while the settlers were farmers, craftsmen and traders. The nomads came to the settlements to exchange animal products for foodstuffs and the other necessities: dates, rice, wheat, clothes, manufactured goods and firearms. The settled people relied on their nomadic allies for military support and to provide transport animals when trading opportunities or military adventures presented themselves.

While some tribes in Arabia, such as the Al Murrah, can claim to have been purely nomadic, these were the exception. Most tribes included nomadic, semi-nomadic and settled members. Over the centuries sections of tribes, sometimes entire tribes, might adopt a settled way of life, while tribal settled people might become nomadic, due to pressures of conquest, drought or disease.

The shaykh or chief of a nomadic tribe might even maintain a permanent base in a settlement, perhaps eventually taking it, while much of the tribe remained nomadic. It was a process like this which led to the establishment of Bani Khalid rule in al-Hasa in the seventeenth and eighteenth centuries. In later times various tribes are known to have maintained permanent camping grounds for the summer months on the outskirts of the oases, most notably the 'Ujman at Hazm west of Mubarraz and Ruqayyiqah south of Hofuf.

Alternatively, a powerful settled clan might extend its influence over the nomadic tribes, as the Jabrids managed to do in the fifteenth century. The outstanding example of this was Al Saud of Dir'iyyah in Najd during the eighteenth century – their influence both supported and was in turn aided by the message of the Reform Movement.

What most distinguished Arabia from the surrounding regions was the fact that the distances and the hardships involved endowed the nomadic bedouin with a potentially significant power. This potential could be realised in conflict with the settled people, but it

Daily life in Hasa and Qatif oases revolved around the great spring pools such as this one, c.1950.

Nomads' camels outside an Eastern Province settlement c.1950.

into being later than the oases and coastal trading settlements of Eastern Arabia. These, as we have seen, are very ancient.

The nomadic tribes of the desert consisted of surprisingly few people – perhaps not so astonishing when one considers the harshness of their environment. The table below was compiled in the first decade of the twentieth century, and shows that even in bygone times in eastern Saudi Arabia the settled population far outnumbered the bedouin. It was only when the settled people lacked organisation or political will that the bedouin were able to take advantage of them. At other times, the logic inherent in the business of establishing law and authority in Arabian settlements – the process of state formation – meant that settled leaders tried to bring the bedouin under their control. In the Eastern Province, the most notable successes were under the Qarmatians, the Jabrids and the House of Saud.

could also flower in cooperation between the two in the use of the trade routes, and the traditional rivalry between nomads and settlers in Arabia should always be seen as disturbances on the surface of the deeper interdependence between them.

The popular view of the nomads sees their way of life as more "primitive", and in some sense less developed, being simpler in its economic base than that of the settlers. In fact, nomadic pastoralism is very specialised. It cannot exist in a vacuum, for nomads have always been dependent on settlements. It is now generally recognised that the true camel-based, highly mobile and tribally organised nomadism of traditional Arabia came

Eastern Province population in the early twentieth century

SETTLED PEOPLES	
Area	*Population*
Hasa Oasis, *including Hofuf (25,000)* *and Mubarraz (8,500)*	67,000
Jinnah island	500
Miyah (Wadi al-)	1,000
Musallamiyah island	2,000
Qatif Oasis, *including Qatif Town* *(10,000)*	26,000
Subaih (Qasr Al)	1,000
Tarut island	3,500
Total settled population	101,000

NOMADIC PEOPLES	
Tribe	
'Ujman	35,000
Hajir, (Bani)	5,000
Khalid (Bani), *after deducting settled* *Bani Khalid on the islands of* *Musallamiyah, Jinnah and Tarut* *and at Qasr al-Subaih, etc.*	10,000
Murrah (Al)	7,000
Total nomadic population	57,000

[From Lorimer *Gazetteer of the Persian Gulf, 'Oman and Central Arabia*, 1908-15]

Farmers of Qatif oasis c.1950.

The nomadic tribes of the Eastern Province

In the several decades since the 1950s, economic changes in the Eastern Province have transformed, probably for ever, the nomadic tribes of the region. From the early days of oil exploration and development, tribesmen were drawn into oil company activities, initially as guides and drivers. Since then, the National Guard has been a major employer, but tribesmen have also been drawn into an increasing variety of other jobs. From the days of King 'Abd al-'Aziz further encouragement has been given to some tribes to settle. For example, the original purpose behind setting up the government farms at Harad was to provide a means for the Al Murrah to adopt the farming life.

Nonetheless, camel, goat and sheep pastoralism continues, though on a much changed basis: absorption into the cash economy, ownership of motor vehicles and water tankers, and the desert wells

An Al Murrah tribesman with his falcon: a traditional sport still popular today.

improved by the government, have all served to transform the old ways.

The bedouin of the Eastern Province in the nineteenth and twentieth centuries have belonged chiefly to the 'Ujman, Al Murrah, Bani Hajir, Bani Khalid, 'Awazim and Mutayr. The 'Ujman and Al Murrah in particular reflect a recurrent feature of tribal history in Arabia: the long-term tendency of tribes to move east and north across the Peninsula towards the Fertile Crescent. These two tribes originated around Najran, perhaps in the eighteenth century. By the time they became powerful in the early twentieth century, the processes of state formation were beginning to circumscribe their autonomy and freedom of movement.

The Al Murrah were renowned among the tribes of Arabia for their way of life, representing as they did an extreme form of nomadism. The Al Murrah tribal territory, or *dirah*, covered the northern and central part of the Empty Quarter south of Hasa Oasis. They had no settled sections, and even their summer wells were not located near settlements. Their annual migrations in search of pasture were sometimes prodigious: the winter rains would usually draw them up to the northern part of the Eastern Province, often as far as Kuwait and southern Iraq. Early summer would find them at their wells along the northern fringe of the Empty Quarter – Yabrin Oasis, Bir Fadhil, Sikak and Nibak – for about three months from June to August, when they would depart for the sands of the Empty Quarter for the autumn grazing. There they would stay until about December, when they awaited

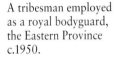

A tribesman employed as a royal bodyguard, the Eastern Province c.1950.

A kid or lamb boiled whole and served on a pile of steaming rice formed the centrepiece of traditional bedouin hospitality. Eastern Province c.1950.

reports of winter rains from the north. If these reports were unfavourable, they might decide instead to move southwest to the Najran area for the winter. An annual round with their camels of 1,900 kilometres was commonplace.

The Al Murrah were held in considerable awe, even among other bedouin, for their skills in tracking and hunting, and their uncanny sense of direction. Their ability to live in one of the most hostile environments known to man depended upon their extreme hardiness and intimate knowledge of the topography and botany of their *dirah*. Less reliant than other nomads on settlers, their pride in their camels amounted to a passion, and the relationship between camel and man to a true symbiosis.

Other tribes of the Eastern Province maintained closer relations with settlers. As we have seen, tribes such as the Jubur (Jabri) and the Bani Khalid might themselves be drawn into the settled life by

becoming sufficiently powerful to control a settlement. This process would often start from their summer camp outside a settlement. Mubarraz may have originated as the summer camp of the Bani

Coffee symbolises hospitality and accompanies the exchange of news and day-to-day decision-making.

Khalid outside Hofuf, and the 'Ujman maintained camps at Ruqayyiqah and Hazm, where they stayed for at least two months *en masse* every summer.

Such tribes developed a more complex economic and social composition than the Al Murrah, since their environment offered more varied opportunities. Settled and semi-settled sections would evolve as members became farmers, traders, or sheep and goat herders. They provided transport services and their numbers gave them a political and military importance.

Their *dirah*s to some extent overlapped, but they each owned sets of desert wells over which they claimed exclusive rights. Like the Al Murrah their camel sections travelled far in search of pasture, but none encroached on Al Murrah territory in the Empty Quarter.

There was a real nobility in the true bedouin, which in some ways justifies the Westerner's – and the settled Arab's – romanticised view of them. The core of it lay in their complete emancipation from the normal concerns of the settler: anxieties over property and the accumulation of wealth. The bedouin conceived property, just as the desert itself and the air that he breathed, as something to fulfil the needs of man, and to be shared with those who lacked it. This attitude lay at the heart of the legendary hospitality which was offered, without question, to complete strangers. The only property they were concerned to accumulate was their herds, and these they regarded as their own only for so long as they could hold onto them: they accepted that they might be deprived of them at a moment's notice by the constant raiding which was to them at once a sport, a lottery, and a means of redistributing a resource of which there was never enough to go round.

The *badawi*'s other source of strength was his profound sense of equality. In the desert there was no division of labour. All men had the same livelihood. Distinctions of wealth could only be so great as could be transported, and in any case were precarious. The shaykh of the tribe was deferred to in his judgments, but only for as long as he commanded the respect of his people. Because nomadic groups were small, and everybody knew each other and understood their business, there was a marked degree of collective consent in

day-to-day decision-making which more complex societies are, by their nature, unable to sustain.

Add to this the nomad's carelessness of life, whether his own or another's – an attitude born of the deprivation and hardships he had constantly to endure – and a truly autonomous figure emerges. Because he expected so little from life, he had an inner freedom to come and go as he pleased, and regarded the ties of settled life, for example of the cultivator or pearl-diver, as unworthy of a man.

In practice, of course, the *badawi* could, and often did, adapt, and could be persuaded to take up a settled occupation. But this choice was based on a sound calculation of the greater benefits that would follow. With the arrival of the oil industry, most bedouin certainly had qualms about giving up the freedom of the desert for a regular day's work. But these misgivings were usually outweighed by the the financial advantages in prospect.

Tribesmen and workers from across the region were drawn into the Eastern Province's oil industry from the early days. Ras Tannurah, 1946.

The settled areas

Before modern times, settlement in the Eastern Province was almost entirely confined to the towns and villages in the two great oases of al-Hasa and Qatif. These oases represented a fascinating confluence of two groups: the ancient non-tribal settled population of the Gulf Coast, who mingled with the tribespeople of inland

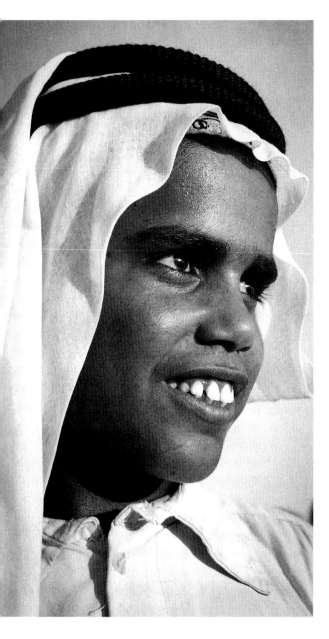

the *'ulama* – whose role was to advise the ruler and administer the law in civil cases. There was therefore great pressure on the ruler to take his responsibilities seriously.

His role in a settlement was considerably more complex than in a nomadic tribe. Like his nomadic counterpart, he was expected to protect the poor from oppression by the rich and powerful, but in a great manufacturing, trading and agricultural centre like Hasa Oasis, with its merchants, landowners, artisans and cultivators, he had also to ensure the smooth running of the economy. This meant that the protection of property had to be balanced against the protection of the weak. Nonetheless, a good ruler would still uphold the claim of the pearl-diver against the captain, or the cultivator against the landowner, if he saw fit.

Public order came top of the ruler's priorities. Part of this involved protecting the settlers from the bedouin. With the help of his advisers, he meted out justice. Punishment was swift and could be severe – flogging, amputation or execution. For enforcement purposes he might maintain a small bodyguard which acted as a police force. Foreign relations were his to conduct, unless he was himself representative of a greater ruler, as under Al Saud. And, to maintain his functions, the population expected him to levy taxes as a proportion of produce and trade. With the Saudi recovery of the Eastern Province in 1913, two notably successful and conscientious governors were installed in Hofuf and Qatif: Abdullah ibn Jiluwi and 'Abd al-Rahman al-Suwaylim respectively. Ibn Jiluwi made it his business to eradicate bedouin lawlessness and violence towards the settled people, and did so with a rigour that inspired confidence in the merchants, landowners and cultivators alike.

Town and village life in the oases of al-Hasa and Qatif, with its lesser satellites such as 'Ayn Jawan and Safwa, reflected the great antiquity of settlement in the area. Hasa Oasis at the beginning of this century was estimated to have about 67,000 inhabitants, including 25,000 in Hofuf and 8,500 in Mubarraz.

Qatif is a maritime oasis – the biggest on the Arabian shore of the Gulf, and indeed the only significant area of cultivation on the mainland between Kuwait and Dubai.

Its cultural links were with Bahrain Island, the north coast of which was a similar maritime oasis with a similar population, also dependent on pearl-diving and spring-fed agriculture. Its population early this century was relatively small: about 26,000, of whom about 10,000 lived in the town of Qatif and its suburbs, the rest in the seventeen or so villages amongst the gardens and along the shore.

Tarut Island, connected by a ford at low water to Qatif Oasis just north of the Kut of Qatif, had a more varied population than Qatif. Settlement on Tarut is of great antiquity, going back 5,000 years and more. Of its 3,500 people in c.1900, about half lived in Tarut village in the centre of the island. These were Baharinah pearl merchants, divers and cultivators of the extensive groves which even today cover the eastern part of the island. Darin, the port of Tarut, was a fishing and pearling village.

Today Darin is still a fishing port with an active boat repair industry. On the north coast of the island, the village of Sanabis, also very ancient, was home to a large community of Baharinah fishermen and pearl-divers, whose 68 boats formed by far the biggest pearling fleet on the Saudi mainland. Another small village of pearl-divers on the north coast, Fanyah or Zawr, was inhabited by various tribespeople from the southern Gulf.

Merchants, landowners and artisans were concentrated in the towns: Hofuf

eastern and central Arabia. In the absence of outside control, political power in the oases of al-Hasa and Qatif was most often held by a tribal ruler, who controlled the balance between the different groups. This was especially true of Hasa Oasis which, being inland, was wholly within the sphere of the desert tribes.

The ruler of a settlement maintained the same egalitarian approach to the people as the shaykh of a nomadic tribe. He was accessible to all and did not rest on ceremony. While he had the power of life and death over the people, he knew that he could be removed by public opinion which, in a tribal milieu where life was cheap, could mean assassination. Since the Jabrid period in the fifteenth century, there was also another increasingly influential group: the religious scholars and leaders –

Respect for one's elders is fundamental to the cohesion of tribal society and is also upheld in the practice of Islam.

and Mubarraz in Hasa Oasis, Qatif Town in Qatif Oasis. The towns served as markets for the surplus of the oases, specialised craft and manufacturing centres, and government headquarters. With the exception of some of the Omani towns and Bahrain, Hofuf was the most important centre of trade in home-produced foodstuffs and manufactured goods in the whole of eastern Arabia. Unlike Mubarraz and Qatif, it was a spacious, well-built town whose houses, forts and palaces had

considerable architectural merit.

The artisans of Hofuf plied a vigorous trade. They were renowned for the weaving of *bisht*s, the outer cloak worn by men. Small factories of a dozen or more pit-looms turned out the cloth. Tailors were similarly organised. Coppersmiths produced the famous Hasa coffee-pots and other cooking utensils. There were silversmiths, goldsmiths and blacksmiths. Woodworkers made furniture, doors, windows, bowls, saddle frames, well gear,

Bookbinding by hand c.1950.

A potter at Jabal Qarah, Hasa Oasis.

drum frames, crates, bird traps and so on. Leatherworkers made crude shoes and sandals. Quarrying for stone and making lime was carried out everywhere in both oases. The only other specialist craftsmen working outside Hofuf were the potters of Jabal Qarah. Basketry and the weaving of palm-leaf mats were routine crafts in the villages, particularly those around Jabal Qarah. Rugs and leather water-skins were made by the bedouin.

The garden labourers in Hasa and Qatif Oases lived in their villages and went out to the gardens every day. They did not own their own gardens, but worked under a yearly share-cropping contract for the landowner, which involved handing over a fixed amount of produce. This meant that in a good year the gardener might do well, while in a bad year he might have to borrow money or arrange an alteration to his contract. The landowner might well lend a sympathetic ear, as it was in his interest to have a conscientious gardener

looking after his valuable asset. In the case of harsh treatment, the gardener might have recourse to the governor, who was seen as the protector of the weak against oppression and injustice.

Oasis villages might be quite substantial: in 1950 seven villages in Hasa Oasis had over 2,000 inhabitants, including Taraf which had 3,700. The total population of the villages at that time was reckoned at some 72,000. Villages were close to the gardens which they served, but generally stood just outside the edge of the plantation area. Indeed, it seems that, as the edge of the gardens has retreated over the centuries, due to salination and perhaps a long-term decrease in the water supply, some villages have crept with it.

Larger villages were walled. Most houses were built of limestone blocks with a facing of gypsum or mud, though some might be built of mud brick, Najd-style. Narrow streets, mosques and a square completed the set-up. Smaller, poorer villages were unwalled, and often had some *barasti* or palm-frond houses amongst their more substantial houses. Smaller still, some unwalled hamlets were located among the gardens, and these would be chiefly of *barasti* construction.

Some merchants and landowners, particularly after the pacification of the region by Al Saud, built themselves grand summer residences in the cool of their gardens, where they might entertain and spend the summer months. Often of quite elaborate construction, some of these houses, or *qusur* as they were known, even boasted swimming pools.

A *barasti* dwelling in Hasa Oasis.

The only other areas of settlement in the Eastern Province were tribal. Settled portions of the Bani Khalid occupied the islands of Jinnah and Musallamiyyah just off the Gulf coast. Jubail, the great new in-

The mosque in the ruined, walled mud village of Tuhaymiyyah, Jabal Qarah, Hasa Oasis.

dustrial city, was a traditional fishing village when the American oilmen arrived in 1933, but did not exist thirty years before. Tribal settlements in semi-desert areas might spring up quickly in response to

economic or political circumstances, and as quickly vanish again.

Such a temporary settlement was Qasr al-Subaih, about six kilometres inland near Jubail. In 1905 sections of the Bani Khalid re-built an old fort there and established a *barasti* village of 350 houses and about 1,000 people – a sizeable settlement. It served as a base of operations against the Mutayr and Al Murrah tribes, with whom the Bani Khalid were on bad terms. The settlement was beyond the Ottoman administration, and would have lost its function once Al Saud had established the new order in the Eastern Province after 1913.

The small but important tribal settlement of Nta' in the Wadi al-Miyah stood

An old garden residence, Jabal Sha'ban, Hasa Oasis.

about half-way between Hasa Oasis and Kuwait, and its people were drawn from the 'Ujman, 'Awazim, Bani Khalid, Mutayr, Rashaydah and Southern Sham-

mar tribes. About 250 houses and four mosques were surrounded by a wall and a few date groves. Three other smaller villages – Mulayjah, Sarrar and Kahafah – occupied the wadi, a broad tract about 150 kilometres long running north-south and affording good grazing grounds for the nomads. With better ground-water than its surroundings, Wadi al-Miyah at different times in history has supported the great pre-Islamic town of Thaj, and, after 1913, a concentration of *Ikhwan* villages such as Hinna, near Thaj, and Sarrar.

An outdoor *majlis* at Safwa, c.1937.

The towns

Hofuf

Hofuf, traditionally the chief town of inland eastern Arabia, stands at the southwestern corner of Hasa Oasis, about 72 kilometres from the nearest point on the coast, 'Uqayr. It remained the administrative centre of the Eastern Province until 1953, when the radical demographic and economic changes of the oil era made the move to Dammam inevitable.

In recent times the old town was isolated from the palm groves to the east, but there is some evidence that it was once surrounded by them – further evidence of the gradual shrinkage of the plantation area over the centuries.

The old town was walled. Though the wall has now gone, the fort of Qasr Ibrahim with the domed Ottoman mosque retains something of the atmosphere of the old town. The town wall enclosed three quarters, Kut, Rifa'ah and Na'athil. These were further divided into districts. There was no segregation of creed, class or occupation in the town. Prominent merchant families lived in both Rifa'ah and Na'athil, and each quarter had its share of government buildings.

In 1950 the population of Hofuf stood at some 60,000, a considerable increase over the 25,000 estimated in 1905. This in-

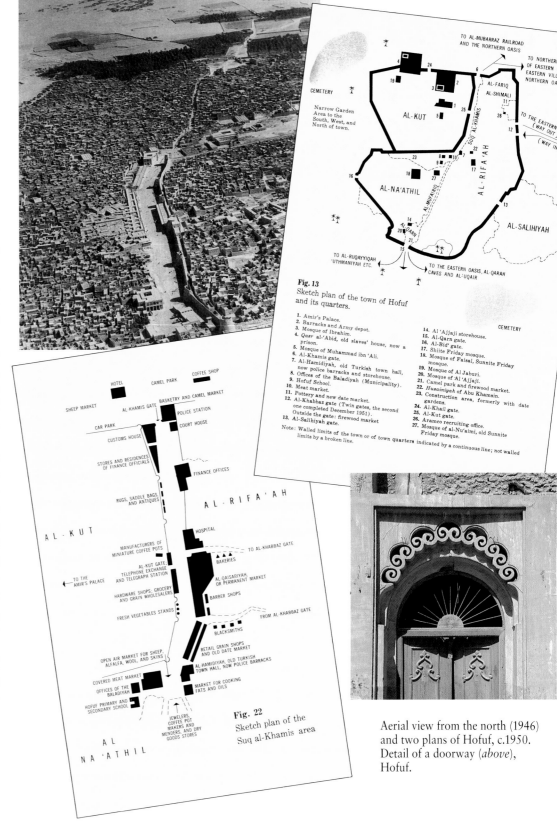

Fig. 13
Sketch plan of the town of Hofuf and its quarters.

1. Amir's Palace.
2. Barracks and Army depot.
3. Mosque of Ibrahim.
4. *Qasr al-'Abid*, old slaves' house, now a prison.
5. Mosque of Muhammad ibn 'Ali.
6. Al-Khamis gate.
7. Al-Hamidiyah, old Turkish town hall, now police barracks and storehouse.
8. Offices of the Baladiyah (Municipality).
9. Hofuf School.
10. Meat market.
11. Pottery and new date market.
12. Al-Khabbaz gate (Twin gates, the second one completed December 1951). Outside the gate: firewood market
13. Al-Salihiyah gate.
14. Al 'Ajjaji storehouse.
15. Al-Qarn gate.
16. Al-Bid' gate.
17. Shiite Friday mosque.
18. Mosque of Faisal, Sunnite Friday mosque.
19. Mosque of Al Jaburi.
20. Mosque of Al 'Ajjaji.
21. Camel park and firewood market.
22. *Husainiyah* of Abu Khamsin.
23. Construction area, formerly with date gardens.
24. Al-Khail gate.
25. Al-Kut gate.
26. Aramco recruiting office.
27. Mosque of al-Nu'aimi, old Sunnite Friday mosque.

Note: Walled limits of the town or of town quarters indicated by a continuous line; not walled limits by a broken line.

Fig. 22
Sketch plan of the Suq al-Khamis area

The Suq al-Khamis or Thursday Market was the hub of commercial life in Hofuf. Famed throughout eastern Arabia for its local and imported goods, it is shown here from the south in 1917 – before the Qaysariyyah Market was built.

Aerial view from the north (1946) and two plans of Hofuf, c.1950. Detail of a doorway (*above*), Hofuf.

crease – a reflection of growing prosperity and stability during the years since the restoration of Saudi rule in 1913 – was accommodated chiefly by building in the gardens within the walls, and by the beginnings of development outside them. The Ottomans had begun this process with the grid-plan layout of the suburb of Salihiyyah. During the twentieth century the process continued with the bedouin camping ground of Ruqayyiqah, overlooked by Qasr Khuzam, becoming permanently settled by a mixture of tribespeople.

The Kut, occupying the northwestern corner, was in a sense a town within a town, a strongly fortified enclosure with thirty bastions which formed the seat of government and the military – a not unusual arrangement in an Arabian, or indeed an Islamic town. The wall of the Kut was much thicker and taller than the main city wall, and was once surrounded by a ditch. Within was the governor's palace and the official guest house. Qasr Ibrahim served as a barracks and administrative quarters. Qasr al-'Abid formerly housed the governor's servants, but came to be used as the jail. The Ottomans had maintained the Kut quarter as the exclusive residential area for official personnel, and there had been shops there. Under the Saudis the residential distinction between the Kut and the other quarters disappeared.

Beneath a tower of the Kut quarter, in the Suq al-Khamis, c.1950.

The governor's horses inside the Kut quarter, c.1950. The palace can be seen in the background (*right*) and Qasr Ibrahim with the domed Mosque of Ibrahim to the left. The horses were stabled outside Qasr al-'Abid nearby.

Inside the palace, Hofuf c.1950.

Buildings within the town were chiefly two-storeyed, though some houses had three storeys, arranged round a central courtyard. Building material was roughly masoned white limestone, quarried from the low plateau on which the town was built. This was faced with gypsum plaster, made by burning the local limestone. Sometimes a mud render would be used instead. Roofing beams were of palm trunks, *ithl* (tamarisk) branches or, less commonly, mangrove poles imported from East Africa.

Plaster surfaces, whether interior or round main doorways, might be elaborately carved with geometric designs, and wooden doors and window shutters painted similarly, in styles which echoed influences from both Najd and the Gulf. Further Gulf influence could be seen in the decorative arches to be seen both inside and round the main doors of the better houses. As in Najd, every house had a coffee hearth. The larger houses had their own well, while public wells were available for the rest.

Mubarraz

A mere three kilometers north of Hofuf, Mubarraz is a relatively young town, and was always smaller and less cosmopolitan than its ancient neighbour.

It grew up during the seventeenth and eighteenth centuries out of the camping ground of the Bani Khalid outside Hofuf. Like Hofuf, Mubarraz was entirely surrounded by gardens until the beginning of the twentieth century. In 1905 its population was estimated at some 8,500. By 1950 this had grown to 28,000, still within the walls.

The buildings in Mubarraz were more modest than those in Hofuf, though built in the same manner. Its craftsmen were well-known for their camel saddles and the decoration and repair of fire-arms, but it lacked Hofuf's profusion of manufacturing skills. There was a permanent market, with the main market day – the Suq al-Arba'ah – on a Wednesday.

There was no inner Kut quarter, but it shared with Hofuf another feature: the extra-mural fort adjacent to the large bedouin camping ground. At Mubarraz this was the renowned old Qasr Sahud, famous for the Saudi resistance to the Ottomans in 1799. Today Qasr Sahud stands within the urban area.

The north wall of Mubarraz in 1924.

Qatif

The town proper of Qatif consisted of a single fortified quarter, or Kut, on the sea shore. The Kut, also known as Qal'at al-Qatif or Qatif Fort, contained about 700 houses by the beginning of the century, and its wall provided the only fortification in the town. Outside it, other residential sections had grown up to give a total population of about 10,000. Of these, 5,000 lived inside the Kut. The houses within the Kut were mostly sturdily built of stone and gypsum mortar and were two or more storeys high. The mosque in the Kut had a conspicuous minaret.

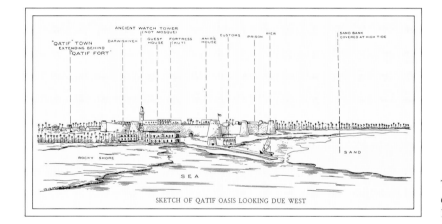

SKETCH OF QATIF OASIS LOOKING DUE WEST

The Qatif waterfront drawn in the 1920s-1930s.

Part of the walled enclosure or Kut of Qatif in the 1930s. In the foreground gypsum or limestone is ready for burning to make *juss* or mortar.

An aerial view of Qatif town before 1950.

A large oasis residence, Qatif, 1948.

The fortifications of the Kut were thought to trace their origins at least to the Qarmatian period. However, the urban fabric of the Kut as we see it in old photographs probably dates from the turbulent times of the sixteenth century. During the Jabrid period in the fifteenth and early sixteenth centuries Qatif's importance is reflected in the name given by some contemporary map-makers to the Gulf: Mare el-Katif, or the Sea of Qatif. In 1520, Qatif was sacked by the Portuguese and their vassals the Hormuzis, and in 1524 the Jabrid rulers fell to Rashid ibn Mughamis of Basra, who in turn was to fall to the Ottomans. Thereafter Qatif became an important prize in the contest between the Ottomans and the Portuguese.

In 1550, the people of Qatif yielded their fortress to the Ottomans, whereupon the Portuguese laid siege to the town, ejecting the Ottomans and destroying the fort. In 1551, the Ottomans returned and built a new citadel there. Qatif became, after Basra, the second base in their campaigns against the Portuguese. However, the Portuguese held on to Bahrain and Hormuz despite Ottoman opposition, and maintained their dominance in the Gulf until 1620. The fort in the middle of Tarut Island is attributed to the Portuguese.

After Portugal lost Hormuz to the British and Persians in 1622, Qatif briefly became a more important centre for Portuguese trade in the Gulf. They came especially for the horses, pearls and dates. The attraction of Qatif lay partly in its fine harbour, which was then one of the best in the Gulf. However, by the early twentieth century, perhaps due to a combination of silting from run-off from the oasis gardens and a falling sea level, only small boats were able to approach. During and after the seventeenth century, Qatif's commercial role was taken over by the Persians on Bahrain, and then by their Omani and Al Khalifa successors there. Local traffic increasingly put into Darin, Ras Tannurah and al-Khobar.

Qatif's *suq* may have had a similarly long history. At the beginning of the twentieth century it was a long, low, covered structure attached to the south-western corner of the Kut, and ran due south for about 400 metres, ending at the suburb of Kuwaykib. The *suq* was built of stone and

In the *suq*, Qatif, c.1950.

Crushing burnt lime or gypsum outside the Kut wall, Qatif, 1930s.

lime, was roofed, and contained about three hundred shops.

In 1871, after two centuries of rule by the Bani Khalid and Al Saud, the Ottomans took over the Eastern Province for the second time, and made Qatif one of three sub-districts in their oddly-named Sanjak of Najd. The other two were Hasa Oasis and Qatar. There were government offices in the Kut, a customs post on the shore, and a garrisoned fort at 'Anik, six kilometres to the south. In 1913, Qatif Oasis as a whole, with its main town, suburbs and seventeen or so villages, and the outlying settlements of Saihat and Safwa, were incorporated once again into the growing domain of the House of Saud.

A street in Qatif c.1948.

Hasa and Qatif: oasis agriculture

Drawing water from an oasis well (*right*)

Hasa Oasis, surrounded by barren desert and fed by its own water sources, is one of the largest true oases in the world. Before the development of recent years it presented an extraordinary sight – large islands of green as far as the eye could see, in complete contrast to the ocean of aridity around. Today this effect has been somewhat diluted, since as much as half of the former cultivated area has been covered by new construction, most of it spreading out from Hofuf and Mubarraz.

The area of cultivated land was in the region of 12,000 hectares. The most reliable estimates of the number of palm trees in such an area stand at around three million. Since the completion of the new irrigation network in the early 1970s, the

potential area of cultivation has been increased by some 19,000 hectares.

Qatif is a maritime oasis. Its people depended upon pearling, fishing, and sea trade as well as on agriculture. Not as large as Hasa Oasis, its irrigated area covered some 4,000 hectares. As in Hasa, there is evidence for considerable shrinkage of the cultivated area since ancient times, when it is thought that settlements outlying today, such as 'Ayn Jawan, Safwa and Sayhat, formed part of a single extended oasis.

The enormous size of the farming area in Hasa and Qatif is made possible by the immense volume of water issuing from subterranean rock strata (the Khobar and Umm al-Radhumah Formations) under natural artesian pressure. In Hasa Oasis the water comes up in some five hundred springs, some of them very large. While many of the smaller springs were privately owned, most, including the largest, were linked to a communal irrigation system. This was necessitated by the sheer volume of water. In 1950 four of the largest springs – Umm Saba', al-Haql, al-Khudud and al-Harrah – each had a flow rate estimated at more than 90,000 litres per minute. Rights to the use of this water were attached not to individuals, but to garden plots, to which the water was led, and from which it was drained away, by an elaborate system of unlined channels.

All the water in Hasa Oasis is warm, and some is hot: over 36°C. Beyond their use as the basis of Hasawi existence, the springs and pools had an important social value as an amenity for relaxation and hygiene. The sulphurous spring at 'Ayn Najm, to the west of Hofuf, used to be a highly regarded resort. In contrast, the water of Qatif is cool.

The basic elements in oasis agriculture in the Eastern Province were water, date palms, donkeys, cattle and alfalfa. The donkeys provided the power for transport and water lifting. Alfalfa was grown everywhere as a highly nutritious fodder for the donkeys and the cattle, both of which provided the manure which was used to fertilise the fields. Manure was carefully collected and spread because, as a true oasis, al-Hasa lacked the annual deposition of fertile silt which was the boon of riverine farming in Iraq and Egypt. Cultivation was all by hand and hoe – ploughs

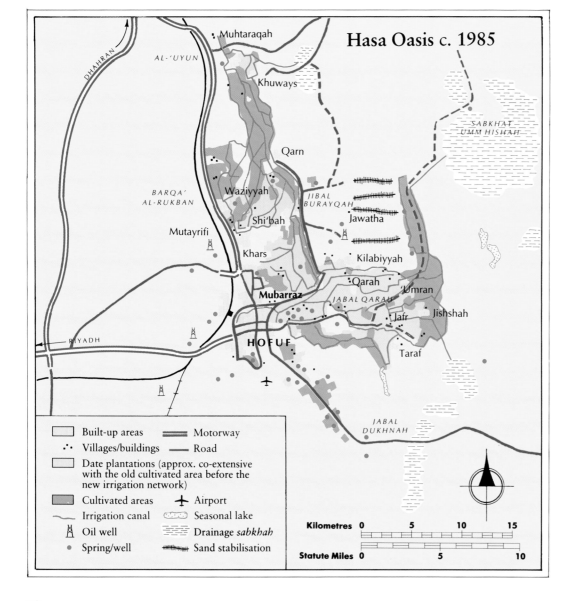

Hasa Oasis c. 1985

Muhtaraqah
AL-'UYUN
DHAHRAN
Khuways
Qarn
BARQA' AL-RUKBAN
Waziyyah
JIBAL BURAYQAH
Jawatha
Shi'bah
Mutayrifi
Khars
Kilabiyyah
Qarah
RIYADH
Mubarraz
JABAL QARAH
'Umran
Jafr
Jishshah
HOFUF
Taraf
SABKHAT UMM HISHAH
JABAL DUKHNAH

Built-up areas | Motorway
Villages/buildings | Road
Date plantations (approx. co-extensive with the old cultivated area before the new irrigation network)
Cultivated areas | Airport
Irrigation canal | Seasonal lake
Oil well | Drainage *sabkhah*
Spring/well | Sand stabilisation

Kilometres 0 5 10 15
Statute Miles 0 5 10

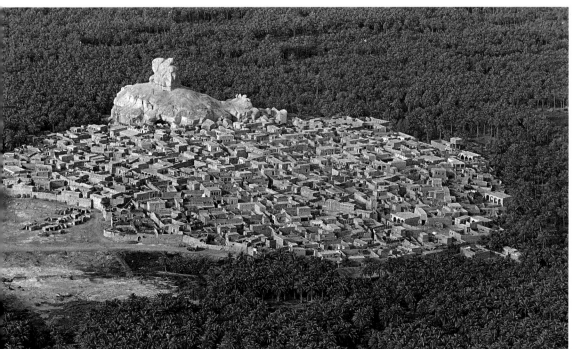

'Ayn al-Khudud, one of the main pools of Hasa Oasis (*above*) was modernised at this time; and the area of cultivation was increased by some 19,000 hectares.

Date-palms surrounding a village (*left*) near Jabal Qarah, Hasa Oasis (1965). Before the new irrigation system, introduced in the 1970s, cultivation covered about 12,000 hectares.

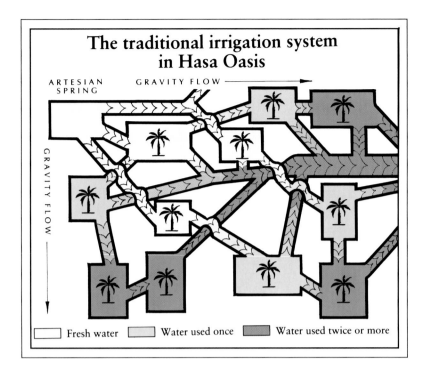

The traditional irrigation system in Hasa Oasis

ARTESIAN SPRING

GRAVITY FLOW →

GRAVITY FLOW

GRAVITY FLOW ↓

Fresh water   Water used once   Water used twice or more

A distribution channel – part of the modern irrigation system in Hasa Oasis.

Today the palm gardens are interspersed with market gardens growing a range of fruit and vegetables such as the potatoes shown here.

were not used – because it had to be intensive and plots were generally small.

Under the traditional system, until the 1970s, the springs fed main channels, some of them, such as Sulaysil, very large and causing some visitors to describe them as rivers. These provided pure water to the first gardens which "drank" from them. The surplus from the first gardens was called "forfeited" water. Having been used once, it was slightly more saline than pure water. "Forfeited" water was drained off to further gardens by secondary channels, several of which might be brought together to form a larger channel. After these gardens, the water would be drained off to further gardens, until the edge of the oasis was reached. Here the final surplus drained away into the sabkhahs which lie to the south-east, east and north-east of the oasis.

The sabkhahs dried out into salt pans during the summer, partly due to the practice of retaining water in the rice paddies during the summer months.

Since the water becomes more saline the more it is used, there was prestige attached to the ownership of plots with a right to pure water. Rigid regulations surrounded the schedule and duration of water available to each plot.

A tithe of produce was traditionally raised in tax from gardens which were irrigated in this way.

From the mid-1960s until 1972, in order to combat progressive salination of the soil and the consequent shrinking of the oasis, the Government substituted a modern distribution system for the old one. This involved distributing only pure water to the gardens, and draining it away without re-using it to outside the Oasis.

Re-structuring involved the construction of several reservoirs with capacities of approximately 55 million litres, and laying out a system of about 3,200 kilometres of concrete channels in order to distribute and drain the water.

As a result, waste and waterlogging were eradicated – much of the water used to soak away in the old unlined channels – and salinity eliminated. The water saved allowed a huge enlargement of the cultivated area to be planned. However, care has to be taken not to over-exploit this non-renewable resource: increased extraction of water by pumps threatens to reduce still further the supply which, the evidence suggests, has been declining gradually since ancient times.

Settled existence in Arabia without the date palm is as inconceivable as the nomad's life without the camel. It was crucial to subsistence, as a source not just of food, but of fuel, fodder and raw material for household items and building. Not only that, it provided the basis for oasis agriculture generally: without the cooler, shadier environment of the palm groves many other plants could not be grown, most especially vegetables and fruits. Date palms have a high tolerance of salinity, and so were ideally adapted to irrigated agriculture in arid conditions.

The date palm (*Phoenix dactylifera*) is

A spring pool in Hasa Oasis, 1937.

'Ayn al-Harrah, Hasa Oasis, 1958, in a partly modernised state. The white donkeys of Hasa and Qatif were famous for their size, strength and endurance. Together with the more numerous ordinary donkeys, they were the primary working animals of oasis life. The white donkeys were often decorated with orange paint made from henna.

known to have been domesticated by 3000 BC in southern Iraq. It is thought that the date palm does not now exist in the truly wild state, yet parts of coastal eastern Arabia support large populations of un-cultivated palms which are not always traceable to formerly cultivated areas or to other activities of man. Perhaps some of these may be modified remnants of the original wild stock, and it is possible that the cultivated forms were developed here in this Arabian Gulf coastal region.

There are some forty or more different varieties of date palm in the Gulf, bearing different varieties of fruit. At least thirty-six varieties are grown in Hasa Oasis, and the Hasawis have always prided them-selves on their quality. The size of Hasa and Qatif Oases has meant that they have traditionally been major exporters of dates. A second traditional cash crop was rice, other produce being grown for local consumption.

The male and female flowers are borne on separate trees. Date plantations consist almost entirely of the fruit-bearing female trees. Farmers practise hand-pollination for a reliable fruit yield.

In Qatif Oasis much, and sometimes all, of the date crop used to be converted into *saluq* and exported for a good profit,

Pollination and harvesting of dates is carried out by hand.

The date harvest, Hasa
Oasis.

especially to India. *Saluq* was a sweet, dry
confection produced by simply boiling
dates, picked at the yellow stage of ripe-
ning, sometimes with added aniseed.
Saluq production in Qatif often necessitated the import of fresh dates from Hasa
Oasis, so maintaining demand and occasionally pushing up prices.

In recent years, with the advent of
affluence and a more varied diet, dates
have fallen out of favour. In contrast, the
demand for tree crops, vegetables and fodder has increased enormously. With

government support, commercial gar-
deners now concentrate on a limited range
of produce in single-crop plots, whereas
under the traditional subsistence pattern a
wide range of vegetables and fruits would
be grown amongst the palms.

The great volume of water enabled both
Hasa and Qatif Oases to grow rice, of a
red variety. Rice cultivation required considerable labour and careful manuring and
flooding. Most locally produced rice was
sold to the bedouin. Other arable crops included alfalfa, the major fodder crop,

are grown commercially in both Hasa and Qatif oases. These include pomegranates, apricots, lemons, limes, figs, peaches, grapes and melons. Mangoes, papaya, bananas and tomatoes are relatively recent introductions. Vegetables are less varied, but there are aubergines, onions, garlic, okra, pumpkins, beans and spinach.

More specialised crops include *mash-mun*, a fragrant herb of the mint family used for make-up, sunflower, sesame, castor oil, mint, aniseed and henna.

The tamarisk tree, or *ithl*, grows everywhere in the cultivated areas of central and eastern Arabia. Its wood is light but strong, and it was used extensively for ceiling rafters.

Maritime life

The Qatif Oasis and its satellites, with Tarut Island, together formed the chief settlement area on the Eastern Province coast. They had an obvious orientation towards the sea; yet because they were also oases, they were untypical of the maritime centres of the Arabian side of the Gulf as a whole. With the exception of the northern coast of Bahrain, they provided the only agricultural district of any extent on the entire Arabian shore of the Gulf between the Shatt al-'Arab in the north and Dubai in the south.

Reliance on maritime resources and skills was accordingly much less than in the other states. Its people developed a culture which was predominantly land-based, but with a maritime dimension: sea-trading, pearling and fishing were all practised, but by a minority, and then often as an adjunct to agriculture.

At different times in the past Qatif had flourished as a port, for example during

Farmers in Hasa Oasis.

which is extremely nutritious and can be cut several times a year. Alfalfa and dates were fed to the famous Hasa white donkeys – a diet which was thought to account for their size, strength and quality.

Amongst the grains, sorghum and millet are the most important, and have been grown since the beginning of oasis agriculture in eastern Arabia. Wheat and some barley were also grown. In years of unusually high rainfall barley might even be planted outside the irrigated areas.

Large quantities of fruit and vegetables

The Customs House at 'Uqayr. At its most basic, 'Uqayr was barely a settlement, acting simply as a protected port of entry for goods bound for Hasa Oasis. When this picture was taken in the late 1930s, it consisted only of a caravanserai, customs post and fort.

the 'Uyunid and 'Usfurid periods in the twelfth, thirteenth and fourteenth centuries. But it lacked good harbour conditions, and Bahrain was always better placed to act as the port of entry for goods from the sea. As a result, Qatif most often acted as a purely local port. The same was true of 'Uqayr which, though it seems to have been an important port in the ninth century and after, for most of its history fulfilled a more limited role as the port for Hasa Oasis.

Pearling

For centuries, probably even millennia, pearling was an important economic activity, perhaps even tracing its origins to the Neolithic period. Pearls have been found in the archaeological record from at least 2000 years ago, in the Jawan tomb, and the Greek author of the *Periplus of the Erythraean Sea*, writing between the first and third centuries AD, noted the extensive pearl fisheries of the Gulf. Pearls were an important export together with dates and horses during the mediaeval period.

During the nineteenth and early twentieth centuries British officials compiled statistical reports on the state of the pearl trade which demonstrate that, before the oil era, the Arab shaykhdoms of the Gulf's southern shore were overwhelmingly dependent on it. The pearl banks of the Gulf were renowned worldwide for the quality and quantity of their pearls, which were traded, via Bombay, to the fashion houses of Europe and America.

In 1907 it was estimated that some 4,500 boats and 74,000 men were en-gaged in pearling in the Gulf, and that the export of the pearls brought at least £1,500,000 (1907 value) annually into the region. By the 1920s these figures had increased, with perhaps half a million people dependent on the divers. Manamah, the capital of Bahrain, had become the centre of the pearl trade, and some pearl merchants became extremely wealthy.

In the 1930s this trade was undermined by the introduction of the cultured pearl. The blow to the economy of the Arab shaykhdoms of the Gulf would have been a crippling one, had it not been for a far more valuable resource, the discovery of which was providentially taking place at the same time. In the event, the oil was to prove far more significant for the people of the Gulf. Ironically, oil, in replacing pearls, was to continue the tradition of most of the Gulf states as single-commodity economies.

Both the diving and the trade were dominated by Kuwait and Bahrain – not surprisingly, as the richest pearl banks were to the north and east of Bahrain. The pearl banks on the Arabian side were free to all, regardless of tribe or nationality, unlike those on the Iranian side. From 1853 Britain assumed responsibility, under the terms of the Perpetual Treaty of Peace, for resolving disputes among the shaykhdoms of the southern Gulf, and maintaining maritime calm. In 1861 Bahrain was brought into the same arrangement. Disputes on the pearl banks died out, and the trade benefited greatly. Britain also discouraged competition from foreign ventures anxious to introduce new diving techniques. The result was that, by the early decades of the twentieth century, under British protection and with demand high, the pearl trade was prospering as never before.

The source of all this was, of course, the divers themselves. During the season their life aboard the boats was grindingly hard, with long hours, a poor diet and the risk of lung and ear diseases and drowning. Each boat carried between ten and forty, including crewmen, divers, haulers-up, assistants, a cook-cum-factotum and the *nakhuda* or captain. In seven cases out of ten the captain owned his boat; other *nakhuda*s hired their boats, or else were employed by the boat owner. The boats were *sambouk*s, *battil*s, *baqqarah*s and *shu'ai*s. Boats of each district formed a fleet which sailed together to and from the banks, with one of the captains appointed by the home ruler as admiral.

The diving season was the hot part of the year, from April till October. It might be divided into greater and lesser diving seasons, and some fleets paid interim visits to their home ports for re-stocking and re-fitting. The depth of a normal dive was between ten and twenty metres, though experienced men might descend as much as forty. Shells were opened first thing the following morning, before the new day's diving began, and the pearls were handed over to the captain.

On reaching port, the captain sold the pearls to a merchant. Out of the money received he would repay loans to moneylenders and merchants taken out at the start of the season. From the profit, one-fifth went to the boat-owner (usually the captain himself) and the season's expenditure on food was deducted. The remainder was divided into shares: three each for the captain and the divers, two for each hauler, and one for each extra hand.

There were a number of tribal divers on the mainland drawn to the fisheries either on a seasonal basis or, like the Bani Khalid on Tarut and Jinnah Islands, who had established permanent settlements. Peaceable and largely illiterate, the Baharinah

Diving from a pearling boat in the Gulf, c.1950. A diver would usually stay down for a minute, occasionally for as much as a minute and a half. A rope was attached to a stone sinker with a noose for his foot and a second rope attached to his waist. One jerk on the second rope acted as a signal to the hauler to bring him up.

were vulnerable to exploitation by unscrupulous captains or boat-owners. The law forbade divers to leave an employer while in debt to him. If anyone did so, his new employer was made responsible for his debt – a strong disincentive to poach another captain's divers. The captains encouraged divers to build up a debt for their food and kit from the start of their first season. Being illiterate, the diver had little means of ensuring he received his full due at the end of the season, and the captain saw to it that he seldom received sufficient to eliminate his debt. In this way the captain kept his divers in his service – caught in a kind of bondage. The rules governing finance, loans and debt favoured creditors and were strictly enforced by a "Diving Court" composed of the shaykh and one or more captains of repute.

While some captains did well, many were squeezed by their own creditors. The local ruler was in a position to take advan-

A pearl diver. He wears a nose pincer and earplugs against the water pressure, leather fingerstalls to protect his hands against abrasions, and a small bag for collecting the oyster shells.

A modern merchant sieving pearls.

The brothers Al-Gosaibi, pearl merchants, examining their stock, 1935.

tage of the trade, and did so by levying a tax on each boat hailing from his port. Those who really profited were the merchants, especially those in Manamah, the most important market in the central Gulf.

Pearls were brought to the merchant or wholesaler (*tajir*) by the captains and the *tawwash*es – petty dealers who went in search of pearls, even on the pearl banks themselves during the season. The merchant sorted pearls out initially by size. Particularly fine ones might be sold individually, but most were divided into 26 quality categories based on colour and shape. These were then sold by the *chau*, a unit derived from weight, and which was confusingly current in different versions in Bahrain, Qatar, Bombay and Poona – a source of complication giving further scope to the clever dealer for profitable transactions.

Though the Hasa coast played its part in the pearling industry, its role was not typical of the purely maritime states. Because of its landward orientation, its oasis agriculture and its productive industries, it was never so dependent on pearling. Statistics collected in 1907 show that its ports contributed a total of 167 boats and 3,444 men to the industry, compared with 9,200 Kuwaitis, almost 13,000 in

Qatar, and over 17,000 Bahrainis. Tarut Island contributed almost two-thirds of the Province's pearling fleet.

The Hasa coast pearling industry also differed in other ways from the Bahraini. As in Qatar, a large proportion of the crews were tribesmen who came to the coast only for the diving season. Never in debt, many used to club together to operate in boats on their own. Boat captains feared the consequences if they tried to cheat them; moreover, such men were free to seek another employer whenever they wished.

The fort of Muhammad Al 'Abd al-Wahhab, a prosperous merchant, Darin, Tarut Island, in 1905. (The gates of the fort are dated 1884.)

Fishing

Fishing was always a small-scale activity on the coast of the Eastern Province – again reflecting its basically land-based subsistence economy. However, a certain amount of fishing was carried on, to satisfy a limited local demand.

Most methods exploited the shallow waters along the coast, particularly those near the rich sea-grass nursery beds of areas like Tarut Bay. They included gill nets and trammel nets, both types designed to entangle fish by their gills. The nets are more than 50 metres long and usually one to two metres deep. They are joined in a long line so that the natural features of the coast tend to guide fish into them. Stake nets are laid in shallow water in creeks and bays, in a circular or spiral shape. The net is hung from stakes, one end often secured ashore. Fish are trapped inside the spiral, and are gilled all along its length.

Off smooth beaches, surrounding nets or beach seines have been in common use down the ages. The net is walked or sailed out and round, depending on its length, and then pulled up on shore. In the shallows, to catch small fish, circular cast nets, two or three metres across, are commonly used. They require great skill to cast.

Fish weirs are a common sight along the Gulf coast. They make use of the tide flow over shallow mud flats and sand banks. They are made from palm or reed stakes set vertically in the water, forming V-shaped structures that end in a small enclosure which traps fish on the ebb tide. Sometimes low stone walls similarly constructed are used instead.

Improvised handspears are still occasionally used to catch basking fish and for fishing along the shallows at night. Simple hand lines are also sometimes used.

In deeper water fishermen use fish pots, once made of palm fronds but today of steel wire. Fish pots are baited and set in water up to ten metres deep. Larger fish are caught by troll lines which are baited lines towed behind the boat.

Fishing continues today in a largely traditional form, modern refinements generally constituting no more than a change in materials. For example, nets used to be made of cotton twine but are today of nylon. The most obvious change

A traditional fishing boat moored at Qatif.

is perhaps the use of in-board and out-board motors instead of sails.

Before the Gulf oil pollution crisis of 1991, government agencies had identified a number of fishery resources in the region which were being exploited by modern trawling methods. Shrimp were being commercially fished by the Saudi Fisheries Company. Today further studies must be carried out to determine the level of exploitable fish stocks.

Boats and boat-building

Traditional craft seen today are almost all of the small *shu'ai* type, adapted for engines and used for fishing or small-scale local transport. In the past, and especially before the arrival of steamships in the Gulf during the mid-nineteenth century, the large cargo-carrying sailing ships of the Gulf were a common sight off the coast. However, the Hasa Coast lacks natural deep-water harbours, and such ships had to anchor off-shore, to be served by small boats. Qatif, for example, could not be approached by boats with a draft of more than six feet, though Darin and Ras Tannurah had deeper anchorages.

It is not surprising therefore that Qatif and Tarut Island lacked the flourishing boat-building industry of Bahrain and Kuwait. Nonetheless, some building was carried on at Darin, where a certain amount of boat repair work can still be seen today.

Methods of boat-building in the past were those common to the Gulf as a whole. Shell construction was used: that is, the planks were bent and fitted together first, on to the keel and stem- and stern-posts, the ribs being fixed later. Hull planking was laid edge-to-edge. The

Fishing with a cast net in the shallows at Dammam.

The old harbour at
Jubail village.

Repairing a *shu'ai* at
Darin, an industry
which still survives
today.

timber used for keel, stem- and stern-posts, hull planking and masts was teak imported from India, while ribs and knees were from natural crooks of timber from the Gulf or elsewhere.

The Gulf coast was the point of departure for some of man's earliest known attempts at long-distance seafaring and certain types of boat-building surviving in eastern Arabia represent the end of a very long tradition of maritime technology. Until the arrival of iron-nailed Chinese ships in the fifteenth century and the Portuguese in the early sixteenth century, the traditional Arabian and Indian Ocean method of construction was to stitch the hull planking together with fibre, a technique which just survives today in some fishing boats of Oman and the South Arabian coast. Hulls were pointed at both ends, the transom stern also being the result of Chinese or Portuguese influence.

The Arab lateen sail was probably an indigenous development in the early centuries AD, being an adaptation of the square sail for sailing close to the wind. The steering oar was used at least until the tenth century, when Arabian seamen invented the rudder-and-rope system, which itself was replaced on transom-sterned craft by the Portuguese-inspired tiller. With the arrival of other European sailing ships, other features were adopted and ships such as the ornate *baghlah*, with its carved poop deck, came into being. Arab seamen were quick to adopt new navigational aids such as the compass (a Chinese invention in the twelfth century) and the sextant.

CHAPTER SIX

The Oil Age

Discovery

IN 1938, after five years of frustrated searching, the American geologists of Standard Oil of California (Socal), decided that Dammam Well no.7 should be drilled "a little bit deeper". This decision – taken in a mood of exasperation at the elusiveness of the treasure beneath the rock strata – was to lead to the discovery of oil in vast quantities. Thus a new era in the Eastern Province and the Kingdom as a whole began.

Dammam Well no.7 continued to produce in its modest way until 1982, and now stands as a monument, touchingly small in scale, to the opening up of the world's largest known oil reserves.

Today the Eastern Province's oilfields, together with the new fields around Riyadh, are thought to contain reserves of 260 billion barrels, or over a quarter of the total known reserves in the world. This figure is constantly being revised upwards as new fields are discovered and extraction techniques are improved. The Kingdom's economic prosperity, its leading role in OPEC and its global economic influence, stem directly from the sheer volume of "black gold" lying beneath the desert and sea of the Eastern Province.

The discovery of the Eastern Province's oil wealth came at an opportune moment, just as the newly formed Kingdom of Saudi Arabia was establishing the apparatus of statehood. The first government agencies were in the process of being formed, Riyadh's early expansion as the capital was under way, and funds were urgently required for the development of the basic infrastructure which would enable the young country to be governed effectively. It was the oil wealth of the Eastern Province which was to provide the means for the Kingdom to transform itself, in little more than forty years, from a traditional, materially backward region of the Middle East into the prosperous modern society of today.

With geological hindsight there seems an inevitability about the discovery and development of oil resources in al-Hasa. Today it seems inconceivable that there should ever have been doubts about their existence there. Yet, ironically, exploration got off to a decidedly shaky start. As early as 1922 Ibn Saud had been alerted to the possibility of oil by the appearance at the 'Uqayr Conference of Major Frank Holmes, an ebullient New Zealand mining engineer who was to play a crucial role in the birth of the Gulf oil industry. This resulted in the granting of a concession to the Eastern and General Syndicate to explore for oil. However, Eastern and General failed to interest any prospectors, and their concession lapsed in 1927. This is one of the most famous lost opportunities of international commerce – yet the decision was reasonable enough given the state of geological knowledge at the time, and the commitments of oil companies in Iraq and Iran.

Max Steineke examining rocks near the Dammam Dome.

Dammam Well no.7, the site of the historic oil strike in 1938.

Holmes had better luck on Bahrain. Here he managed, in 1928, to interest an American company, Standard Oil of California, in taking over Eastern and General's concession. This led, in 1930, to the formation of the Bahrain Petroleum Company, and the discovery of oil on Bahrain in 1932. Socal's geologists were quick to notice that geological formations on the Arabian mainland bore a striking similarity to those on Bahrain. By 1933, Socal had entered into negotiations in Jeddah with King 'Abd al-'Aziz for preliminary investigations and a concession in the Eastern Province. The result was the historic Concession Agreement, drafted by Lloyd Hamilton of Socal, and signed by him and Shaykh Abdullah Sulayman, the Finance Minister in Jeddah, on May 29th 1933.

In November 1933 the concession was assigned to a specially created subsidiary of Socal, the California Arabian Standard Oil Company (Casoc). In 1936 The Texas Company (later Texaco) took a half share of Casoc. This was the company whose name was to be changed, in 1944, to Aramco, the Arabian American Oil Company. Since 1980 the company has been wholly Government-owned and is known as Saudi Aramco.

Casoc appointed the Gosaibi brothers as its agents in al-Hasa, and set up rudimentary facilities at Hofuf and Jubail, then a small fishing village. The first geologists stepped ashore in September 1933, and at once began mapping and prospecting. They soon confirmed the Dammam Dome as a geologically promising feature, and in 1934 decided to test drill. A camp was established on the Dome, near Jabal Dhahran, its most prominent feature. Later the camp became known simply as Dhahran. Equipment was imported from the U.S. into a tiny fishing settlement on the coast called al-Khobar, just south of the small town of Dammam.

Dhahran camp in the early days.

One of the first wells in the Eastern Province.

An exploration vehicle crossing the rocky terrain around Hofuf.

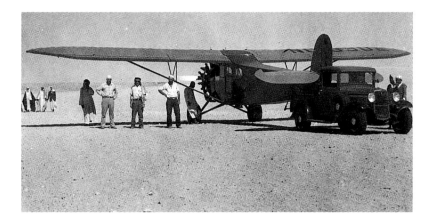

The Fairchild reconnaissance plane, towed by a truck, Jubail, 1934.

The commemorative plaque which now marks Dammam Well no.7.

King 'Abd al-'Aziz with Floyd Ohliger, Casoc's Manager in Residence in Saudi Arabia when Well no.7 struck oil in 1938.

A geological field party near Dhahran, 1936.

Such were the beginnings of the major demographic changes in the Eastern Province which mark the modern era: the shift of population density away from the traditional oases of al-Hasa and Qatif.

This was the heroic age of prospecting in Saudi Arabia. It has given the oil business some of its most renowned figures – Miller, Henry, Hoover, Kerr, Mountain, Steineke and Ohliger among the Americans, and, among the locals, Khamis ibn Rimthan, the legendary 'Ujmani guide, 'Abd al-Hadi ibn Jithina of the Al Murrah, and Salim Aba Rus. Working together, these men fanned out through the Eastern Province, mapping and prospecting as they went. In 1934 they were joined by a reconnaissance aircraft, which revolutionised the rate of their investigations.

These pioneering American geologists and engineers were hardy, resourceful characters who were used to achieving their ends with the minimum of means, improvising as necessary. When they arrived they knew next to nothing of the alien culture in which they found themselves. But they were forthright, adaptable and tough – qualities which they shared with their hosts, and which seem to have inspired a mutual respect. And there was another factor which the Saudis found refreshing: involvement with Casoc and its parent Socal did not, in those days, entail the political dimension which involvement with the British oil companies of the region would have carried.

Khamis ibn Rimthan, the legendary 'Ujmani guide.

Sometimes the heavy Ford automobiles were abandoned in favour of traditional camel caravans for geological expeditions, 1936.

Between 1935 and 1938 ten wells were drilled into the Dammam Dome. The results failed to confirm expectations. Thus the decision was taken, on Max Steineke's advice, to take Well no.7 deeper still, into the strata known as the Arab Formation. In early March 1938 oil began to flow in commercial quantities, at a depth of 1,440 metres. Saudi Arabia had entered the oil business.

This breakthrough was the signal for a major influx of Casoc personnel into the Eastern Province. More accommodation was built at Dhahran, construction began of an oil port next to deep water at Ras Tannurah, where the Ottoman government had once maintained a coaling station, and smaller shipping facilities were developed at al-Khobar. Local labour was recruited and Casoc initiated the process of training a Saudi workforce – a commitment whose long-term results can be seen today in the largely Saudi ised management and workforce of Saudi Aramco. More men meant more prospecting, and Casoc's geologists, under Steineke's direction, began probing the secrets of what were to become the Abqaiq and Abu Hadriya oilfields. By 1940 there were 435 Americans, including some wives and children, together with 3,300 non-Americans, chiefly Saudis.

In these pre-War years the Americans developed a flexible, helpful relationship with the Saudi government. The government in the 1930s lacked both management and technical skills, and regarded Casoc as a friend which could set up and run big projects for it. Casoc responded: hospitals, public health programmes, the drilling of water wells, agricultural projects and transportation all received vital help from Casoc, and after the War Aramco was to continue the tradition on a larger scale.

The construction of the pier at al-Khobar, which was completed (*right*) in 1935, was significant as the first mass employment of the local population by the industry which they were later to run themselves. Using fishing boats, great quantities of rock from the bottom of the Gulf were piled into two parallel walls (*below*), 1934, which slowly stretched out into the water.

The Second World War and after

During 1940-41 Casoc operations were run down because of wartime difficulties. By 1944, however, the lull had been brought to an end by expanding demand for oil for the Allied war effort, and the increased safety of the sea lanes. Casoc was re-named Aramco, expansion was set in hand, and new personnel arrived.

By 1945 a new refinery had been built at Ras Tannurah, together with storage

The customs house at Ras Tannurah, 1947.

tanks, loading lines, a T-shaped pier with tanker berths, and a submarine pipeline to Bahrain. Oil production leapt yearly, from below 20,000 bpd before 1944, to 500,000 bpd in 1949. The first wells were sunk into the huge Ghawar oilfield, later found to be the world's largest single onshore reservoir. Prospecting continued apace, into the Empty Quarter and the Gulf, where the first off-shore field, Safaniyyah, was discovered in 1951.

From now until the 1970s, annual production steadily increased: in 1958 it reached 1m bpd; by 1967 it had passed the

2.5m bpd mark. In an age of small tankers, Aramco cast around for new ways to export such volumes. In the late 1940s, it was decided to proceed with the Trans-Arabian Pipeline. Completed in 1950, this "long steel shortcut" took oil from the Eastern Province to the Mediterranean port of Sidon; despite the political upheavals of the region, its operations continued until the early 1980s.

In the early days, the production of Saudi oil was a relatively simple business. Crude was produced from wells, taken via a network of pipelines to storage tanks on

the coast, and exported. Little was refined at home, and associated gases were burnt off – which, in a less environmentally aware world than today, was normal practice, despite the waste of a potentially valuable resource. It was only as uses and markets for this gas emerged, that Aramco developed the idea of the Master Gas System to collect and process it – a major undertaking which was launched in the 1970s.

The transformation of the company into the world's largest oil producer involved, in 1948, a widening of its ownership: Exxon and Mobil took 30 per cent and 10 per cent respectively, 30 per cent each remaining with Socal and Texaco. So it remained until 1973, when the Saudi government acquired a 25 per cent interest, later increased to 60 per cent in 1974 and, in 1980, to 100 per cent.

Less than fifty years after Casoc's formation this company, now known as Saudi Aramco, was being run by the sons and grandsons of a traditional, largely tribal people. The Saudi element was vital from the start, and was encouraged by Aramco's vigorous training programmes. By the 1950s general schooling was also available for company employees who, as their education skills increased, rose stead-

Ras Tannurah refinery, 1946/7.

ily to more responsible positions. By 1957 Saudis already made up 70 per cent of Aramco's 18,325 employees. By 1967 they held 57 per cent of the company's 1373 managerial or supervisory posts. Employees were sent abroad on scholarships for further training. In 1963, the University of Petroleum and Minerals was established as a college at Dhahran, being given university status in 1975. Today, as the King Fahd University of Petroleum and Minerals, its student enrolment stands at some 14,000, and it is at the cutting edge of

The expatriate camp at Ras Tannurah (c.1950) formed the centre of the international community.

The construction of the Dammam-Riyadh railway
(*above*) began in 1947. A Saudi freight train passes
Jabal Madhra' en route to Dhahran, 1958.

research into new technologies for the oil industry. As a source of professionals to man the nation's industry its reputation is unrivalled.

In addition, Aramco ran a home ownership scheme to enable employees to build their own houses, and encouraged employees to set up in business on their own. In the 1950s and 1960s the local economy was much assisted by Aramco departments – the Local Industrial Development Division, and the Agricultural Assistance Division – specifically set up to foster its growth. Some of the best-known names on the Saudi business scene, such as Bin Laden, originated in this way.

The development of oil as an export commodity had an inevitable effect on the economy and culture of the Eastern Province as a whole. In a generation its economic base was to be transformed. Its absorption into the global marketplace

had an enormous and continuing impact on the horizons and expectations of its people. Private development of houses and businesses was complemented by government spending on communications, health, hospitals, water, drainage and agriculture. The growth of the new centres of population – Dammam, Dhahran, al-Khobar – accelerated rapidly, to such an extent that, in the 1950s, the traditional predominance of Qatif and Hasa Oasis was eclipsed. Reflecting this shift, the Governor of the Eastern Province, Amir Saud ibn Abdullah ibn Jiluwi, moved the administrative headquarters of the Province from Hofuf to Dammam in 1953.

In keeping with Casoc's pre-war policy, Aramco also provided direct help to the government. The chief example of this was the construction of the 580-kilometre railway from Dammam to Riyadh. Started in 1947, the railway was completed in 1951,

with Aramco as project manager. The railway still functions, but its role today gives little indication of its great significance

King 'Abd al-'Aziz with Crown Prince Saud, examines the golden spike and mallet before driving in the last rail (October 1951).

before the advent of roads and regular air travel. More than anything else, the railway opened up the interior to imports from the Gulf. At a stroke it became possible to import large pieces of equipment and modern building materials. In fact, the opening of the railway signalled a new phase in the development of Hofuf and Riyadh: henceforward more and more new building was done in concrete and steel. The appearance of towns changed accordingly. They also expanded as workers were drawn to them, while the security brought by central government meant that expansion outside the towns was now possible, given the availability of water.

These were the years when the implications of the discovery began to be understood and the shape of the landscape began to change, forever. But for a short time only, the old and the new existed alongside each other and were recorded in the photographs of those who lived and worked in the region.

The radio communications centre, Jubail c.1950 (*right*). For a while fishing continued to be the main activity in the old town of Jubail (*below*. Young citizens of the new Saudi Arabia (*opposite*) enjoying the shade in front of the traditional architecture of Salih Islam house, Dammam, 1965.

CHAPTER SEVEN

The Eastern Province Today

The urban centres

THE historic towns and villages of Hasa Oasis, Qatif and Tarut Island are still important centres. But since World War II they have been eclipsed by the new conurbations.

The impetus for this skilfully guided transformation has been the oil and gas industry. In the old days Dammam, al-Khobar and Jubail were small fishing villages. Dammam is now the administrative and commercial capital of the region, and the Kingdom's third city. Al-Khobar merged into a single municipal authority with Dammam and Dhahran in 1982 and is now part of a virtually continuous coastal conurbation. And Jubail, the most recent of the new cities – set up by government initiative during the late 1970s – is the most dynamic industrial centre on the Gulf. There has been a population explosion during the last few decades and there are now thought to be one and a half million living in the region, with over 80 per cent in the new conurbations.

In working this transformation man has imposed himself on the landscape in dramatic fashion. The process of building the new cities on the soft, gently shelving coastline entailed Herculean earth--moving efforts, especially at Jubail. Large stretches of the coastline have been altered – in some cases for amenity value, as with the new Jubail and Dammam-al-Khobar corniches and Half Moon Bay, and in others for economic reasons, as with the oil terminal at Ras Tannurah, the port expansion at Dammam, and the new port and industrial installations at Jubail. A new network of roads is in place, including the impressive King Fahd Causeway which links the Eastern Province with Bahrain. The new King Fahd International Airport, is located 36 kilometres northwest of Dammam.

While Jubail is a unique phenomenon in the Eastern Province – a new city created to fulfil a specific function in the national economy – the other cities have grown spontaneously, and over a longer period of time. The old towns of Hofuf, Mubarraz and Qatif, with their long history as traditional centres, owe their rapid growth to the modern economy. But sound planning and thoughtful administration have kept these deep-rooted communities intact. By contrast the Dammam-al-Khobar-Dhahran conurbation, the capital area of the Eastern Province, derives its very existence as the political and commercial centre from the oil discoveries of the 1930s.

In the past, approximately a third of the Eastern Province's people were town-dwellers, the remainder being divided between settled cultivators and the nomadic bedouin tribes. Today the overwhelming majority of people live in towns, accustomed to the comforts and amenities of city and suburban life. Weekend relaxation might include a day at the beach, water-skiing, swimming, fishing, or picnicking with the family. A strong sense of tradition prevails despite the advent of the oil industry.

◀ Jubail Industrial City is widely acclaimed as a pioneering example of Islamic and industrial town planning.

The King Fahd Causeway which links Saudi Arabia to Bahrain spans shallow sea. Here the largest reclaimed section is more of an artificial island: it has a customs post and coastguard facilities.

Dammam, al-Khobar and Dhahran

Until the early 1980s Dammam, the capital of the Eastern Province since 1953, was still a separate city, but so close to al-Khobar and Dhahran that it took only a few minutes to travel between them. In 1982 they were merged into a single entity, known today as the Dammam Area, to be administered by a single municipal authority. Together they cover a total area of 718 square kilometres. They have, however, retained their distinctive characters and, indeed, their own local administrations. The total population of the Dammam Area is estimated at around 400,000 with an annual growth rate of 3.6 per cent.

With its two large industrial estates, Dammam is the principal marketing and industrial centre of the Eastern Province –

and the third largest in the Kingdom after Riyadh and Jeddah – although almost all primary hydrocarbon-based industries are concentrated in Jubail.

There are, moreover, two major landmarks signposting Dammam's modernity and economic strength.

- The King Abdul Aziz Port is one of the Kingdom's largest and busiest. Having grown organically to serve the rapidly expanding business of the Eastern region, it was also to become the gateway for most of the imports and exports of the Central Province and Riyadh itself.

- The Dammam-Riyadh Railway was one of the accomplishments of King Abdul Aziz himself, an essential part of the transport and communications network linking the interior of the Kingdom with

the perimeter and the world beyond.

Dammam is also characterised by a number of distinctive modern structures. Among the most striking of these are the Coastal Centre, established for sea sports by the General Presidency of Youth Welfare, and the King Fahd Park, a 250 square metre resort comprising fountains, fenced lawns, ponds and expansive flowerbeds.

Before the discovery of oil, al-Khobar was a fishing and pearling village with a small dhow trade with Bahrain. Today its population is around 120,000, and growing fast, at a rate of 6.8 per cent per year. It is regarded with affection by its residents who value its relatively quiet and relaxed atmosphere. It is a lively commercial and shopping centre and has a certain amount of industry, though not

Some of the innovative monuments which enliven the corniche in Dammam.

on the scale of Dammam, fifteen kilometres up the coast. Its dhow transport link with Bahrain has been made redundant since the opening of the King Fahd Causeway in 1986. Twenty-five kilometres long, this aerial motorway incorporates a man-made island stop-over at the centre point, housing the customs and immigration facilities for both Saudi Arabia and Bahrain.

Dhahran, which is the inland point of the triangle and only ten kilometres from al-Khobar and Dammam, is less a city than a combination of three important institutions:

-The headquarters of Saudi Aramco, itself a self-contained and enclosed urban entity on the site of the original Aramco township which is still a living part of the greatly expanded complex.

- The King Fahd University of Petroleum and Minerals, the Kingdom's leading technical institution and a world centre in its field. Specialist areas of study include engineering, industrial management and environmental design. The Applied Research Centre, based at the university, contributes to the efficient appliction of modern technology across the Kingdom.

- King Fahd International Airport: the vast replacement for Dhahran International Airport, which was itself the first major airport in the Kingdom. With a capacity of up to 10 million passengers annually and a site spread across some 760 square kilometres, this new airport comprises a key infrastructural facility for future expansion in the Province.

Government

The Kingdom is governed according to Islamic precepts under which it is the Government's responsibility to provide whatever utilities and services are considered necessary for the well-being of the people. This means being responsible for education, health, housing and social welfare; it also means investing in the oil and gas industries, which are mostly state-owned, and also in the primary and secondary industries.

These investments have been guided by a series of Five-Year Plans, initiated in 1970; the annual budget is determined by the level of oil revenue and the amount of Government borrowing. The Five-Year Plans originally focused on the need for an infrastructure and on the development

105

of the oil industry. Now that these are in place, the emphasis has been very much on the development of secondary industries and increased privatisation. Many of the Kingdom's products are now exported throughout the world.

The structure of Government is based on thirteen regional divisions or Governorates in Riyadh. Various ministries have field offices in the provinces, but these, together with local development and administration, the maintenance of law and order and the implementation of Shariah judgements, are entrusted to a local Governor or Amir, appointed by the Ministry of the Interior in Riyadh. The Eastern Province's status as the pillar of the Kingdom's economy and one of its most populous regions is recognised by the appointment of Prince Muhammad ibn Fahd, son of His Majesty King Fahd ibn 'Abd al-'Aziz, as Governor, based in the provincial capital Dammam.

A water tower in Qatif.

The Rajheyah Mosque in Qatif (*left*) is a fine example of traditional Islamic architecture.

Young palms along the new corniche in Qatif.

Suburban villas in al-Khobar (*opposite*) and Qatif (*right*); the privacy of the family is maintained by high compound walls.

In the gold suq, Dammam (*left*).

The Thursday Market, Hofuf (*right*), preserves something of the atmosphere of former times.

Buying cloth, al-Khobar (*below*), this kind of shopping can still be a social occasion.

Supermarket shopping has introduced foods from all over the world, transforming the local diet.

Al Rushaid Village, al-Khobar (*right*), typifies company housing, providing all the comforts and amenities required by the expatriate.

A view of al-Khobar
(*right*).

Today various forms of
civic art enliven the
urban landscape. A
mural in al-Khobar
(*left*), a restaurant at
Half Moon Bay, south
of Dammam (*top left*).

This sculpture
(*above*)
commemorates the
voyage of the first Arab
astronaut, Prince Sultan
ibn Salman ibn 'Abd al-
'Aziz Al-Saud, as a
payload specialist on
NASA's shuttle in 1985.

The Sheraton hotel in
Dammam.

A residential area in
Dammam.

Dammam stadium *(below)*
is a landmark on the city
skyline.

The Eastern Province Chamber of Commerce headquarters (*opposite*) has become a landmark on fire Al-Khobar-Dammam highway.

Dhahran: home to the internationally renowned King Fahd University of Petroleum and Minerals (*far right*), to Dhahran International Airport (*right*), and also to the Saudi Aramco headquarters complex where the Dhahran Mosque (*below*) is located. All three institutions have been acclaimed for their impressive, contemporary Islamic architecture.

Social welfare

The Kingdom's commitment to the welfare of the whole community is evident from the enormous budgets allocated to health, education and housing. During the Second, Third and Fourth Five-Year Plans (1975-1990) huge sums were spent on construction and setting up the basic infrastructure. Schools, universities, hospitals and health centres spread throughout the Kingdom, not least in the Eastern Province, and generous grants of land and interest-free loans were made to individuals who wished to build their own homes.

Latterly the emphasis shifted to efficient management of a system which, in physical terms, was largely complete, and to the provision of trained teaching and medical staff. Increasingly, highly qualified Saudis are filling the posts.

Health

The Eastern Province is divided for administrative purposes into two health districts: the Hasa Health District, covering Hasa Oasis and inland areas, and the Eastern Province Health District, covering the more recent population centres – Dammam, al-Khobar, Dhahran, Qatif and Jubail and their areas – along the coast.

By the 1990s, the Eastern Province Health District provided about 1,700 beds in ten hospitals. These included special centres for chest diseases and paediatrics.

Jubail's hospitals provide a wide range of health services, including accident and emergency cover.

Two new hospitals were being planned for Dammam and Khafji. The King Fahd University Hospital in al-Khobar, run by King Faisal University, al-Hasa, as part of its medical faculty, served as a training hospital. The Hasa Health District had four hospitals providing almost 700 beds. In the public health sector as a whole, approximately 1,000 doctors and a further 8,000 medical staff, were employed.

Preventive medicine has played a key role in the Kingdom's health policy, and its message is spread through the network of primary health care centres and mobile clinics. The Saudi Red Crescent Society runs thirteen first aid centres in the Eastern Province, and provides assistance to military medical teams. Care and rehabilitation of the mentally and physically handicapped has always played a central role.

Public health provision is matched by private health care, which is actively encouraged through grants of land and generous loan arrangements by the Ministry of Health, which also supervises it. In the Eastern Province, private sector hospitals today provide almost as many beds as the public sector.

Social insurance

The General Organisation for Social Insurance (GOSI) supervises safety at work and guarantees generous compensation to employees, the self-employed and their families, regardless of nationality, for permanent and temporary disability due to sickness, injury or maternity. GOSI also pays old age pensions and death benefits. Its revenues are drawn from a mix of employers' and employees' contributions, investments and Government subsidy.

Education

Saudi Arabia has spared no expense in implementing free universal education. Equal emphasis is placed on female and male education, which – except at the kindergarten level – are as strictly segregated as other areas of life outside the home.

The Ministry of Education has its main regional department in Dammam and another in Hofuf. As elsewhere in the Kingdom, schooling is divided into three stages: primary (*ibtida'i*), intermediate (*mutawassit*) and secondary (*thanawi*). The primary stage lasts six years, ending with an examination. The intermediate stage lasts three years, ending with another examination leading on to the secondary stage of three years, which culminates in the Saudi Baccalaureat (the *tawjihiyyah*). After one year at secondary school, the pupil is offered the choice of scientific or arts streams.

At the post-intermediate level there are schools for those not wishing to proceed to secondary level. These are high-grade vocational schools, which offer courses in teaching, scientific and technical skills, agriculture, and business studies. Technical training is also provided by the many vocational training centres run by the General Organisation for Technical and Vocational Training, which works with the Ministry of Labour and Social Affairs. Other organisations too, such as the National Guard and Saudi Aramco, run their own training schemes.

The Eastern Province has two of the Kingdom's seven universities: the King Fahd University of Petroleum and Minerals in Dhahran, and the King Faisal University in Hofuf and Dammam. Several other local institutions are affiliated to the King Faisal University including the King Fahd University Hospital in al-Khobar and in Hasa Oasis the Hasa and Dammam Computer Centre, as well as research centres studying date palms, camels and water resources.

Dammam Public Library also houses the regional Department of Antiquities and its museum.

Hasa Oasis has a long history of traditional learning and teaching, particularly in Qur'an studies, and was well known for its scholars in the seventeenth and eighteenth centuries. Today Hasa Oasis has some 180 schools like the one above, Dammam (*right and below*) has more than a hundred schools.

The campus of King Fahd University of Petroleum and Minerals (*left and opposite*) is a self-contained community with its own infrastructure, including the water-tower which dominates the scene (*opposite, bottom*).

The King Fahd University of Petroleum and Minerals, Dhahran (**KFUPM**)

KFUPM occupies a prominent position atop a limestone *jabal* in Dhahran. It was founded as a college in 1963 with under 100 students. By 1974 it had increased its intake to 1,500 students, and in 1975 was raised to university status. KFUPM is an autonomous institution, with the Minister of Higher Education as Chairman of its board. Degrees at Bachelors and Masters level are offered in Engineering (Civil, Mechanical, Electrical, Chemical, Petroleum, Architectural and Systems), in the Sciences (Mathematics, Geology, Physics and Chemistry), and in Industrial Management and Environmental Design. Ph.D.'s are offered in various branches of Engineering, and in Chemistry. Courses are taught in English.

By 1987 student enrolment had reached over 14,000, and Saudis accounted for 45 per cent of teaching staff. The economic downturn of the mid-1980s caused KFUPM to trim its intake, but it has now returned to previous levels.

KFUPM's priority is, and always has been, to prepare students for the exacting demands of the Kingdom's oil and gas industries. It now has a worldwide reputation, and attracts foreign students from over fifty countries. Its large campus includes over one hundred laboratories, research facilities and residential accommodation.

Sport, Youth Welfare and Recreation

Sport and Youth Welfare are the responsibility of the General Presidency of Youth Welfare, with its regional headquarters in Dammam. It promotes the well-being of the nation's youth, placing particular emphasis on sport (football is followed with enthusiasm) and other forms of healthy recreation, and encouraging an interest in the Kingdom's history and traditions.

In the cities it is common practice to picnic in the urban parks and recreation areas and along the Dammam-al-Khobar Corniche.

On the beach at Dammam (*above*); a squash rackets match played at one of the sports centres provided by the Presidency of Youth Welfare; families on a Friday afternoon, Jabal Qarah, Hasa Oasis (*opposite*).

The economy

The Eastern Province's oil fields are estimated to contain reserves of at least 260 billion barrels – sufficient for 150 years at present production rates, and around a quarter of total known world reserves. Known gas reserves stand at over 5,000 billion cubic metres. Such figures give the Eastern Province immeasurable economic significance, which was underlined by the international response in 1990 to the threat posed by Iraq's occupation of Kuwait.

Over recent decades the Saudi economy has weathered a number of changes. The boom of the 1970s and early 1980s was followed by a drop in the price of oil which meant the Kingdom incurred a deficit. This had to be financed by drawing on reserves and later by borrowing. As a result, Government policy began to place more emphasis on diversification away from oil and raw material production into higher value-added, down-line products for the domestic, Gulf and overseas markets.

These developments led to a revival in the economy: the Saudi stock market boomed at the end of the 1980s, reflecting investor confidence. Many of the industries now based in the Eastern Province are privately owned. Foreign joint venture participation is actively encouraged in larger enterprises to bring in both investment and technology from abroad. The diversification effort is already having a major impact on the Eastern Province, which contains, at Jubail and Dammam, two of the five main industrial zones in the Kingdom (the others being Riyadh, Jeddah and Yanbu).

Oil production began to recover in the late 1980s and by early 1990 had risen to 5 million barrels per day (bpd). The Kingdom's aim is to create a stable oil market irrespective of political upheavals in the Gulf. Stability of price and supply will enable consumer and producer to plan for the future with confidence.

The invasion of Kuwait in August 1990 created a challenging situation: the Kingdom's Government was determined to maintain worldwide stability in the oil markets. In order to do so, production had to be increased rapidly. A number of Saudi Aramco's facilities were recommissioned and plans for new projects stepped up. Oil production rose to 8.5 million bpd which kept the international oil price relatively low. Government revenues from oil surged, but this was swallowed up by the cost of the war.

Throughout the crisis "business as usual" was the watchword, particularly in the Eastern Province. Large numbers of foreign personnel had to be catered for and back-up supplies of fuel, water and other essentials provided. No shortages were reported and the coalition forces commended the efficient distribution of fuel by Samarec (the Saudi Arabian Marketing and Refining Company). To facilitate this, several kilometres of new pipelines together with new loading terminals were constructed.

After the war, oil production levels remained high in response to increasing demands across the world. Expansion plans for the Eastern Province's hydrocarbon resources would lead to a capacity of 10 million bpd by the mid-1990s. Business confidence was high; private capital was being invested in primary and secondary industries; for the first time private Saudi investors became involved in the oil business when, early in 1992, some joined in a venture with the Fina oil company to supply crude to Fina refineries in the USA. Jubail boomed as SABIC (Saudi Arabian Basic Industries Corporation) expanded its industries and more residential housing was built to accommodate the estimated 10,000 more workers who would be required later in the decade. Eastern Province firms readied themselves to help in the reconstruction of Kuwait.

As moves to create a Common Market among the Gulf Cooperation Council states (Kuwait, Saudi Arabia, Bahrain, Qatar, the United Arab Emirates and Oman) gather pace, the Eastern Province still dominates industrial development in the Gulf. In 1991, the GCC licensed over 600 projects with a total investment of more than $4 billion; of this $2.5 billion was accounted for by projects in Saudi Arabia.

These policies have already played their part in the economic story of the Eastern Province. They will continue to contribute to its success, as long as the stability of the Gulf region can be ensured, and large production volumes of oil and gas can be maintained, with a stable pricing regime.

Oil and gas

The Eastern Province contains oil reserves of at least 260 billion barrels. This figure is being revised constantly upwards as reservoir engineering and extraction techniques improve, so that many experts believe that a truer estimate stands at well over 300 billion barrels, or one-third of known world reserves. Gas, too, is found abundantly, in association with the oil, at a ratio of approximately fifteen cubic metres to each barrel of oil, and there are estimated to be more than 5,000 billion cubic metres of gas reserves.

All the Eastern Province oil and gas fields and facilities are owned by the Government and operated by Saudi Aramco, except for those in the Divided Zone shared with Kuwait, where the onshore concession is held by the Getty Oil Company, and the offshore concession by the Arabian Oil Company Limited. Since 1980, Saudi Aramco has been wholly Government-owned; its former multinational partners continue to supply expertise and have special access to its oil products.

Saudi Aramco is both the world's largest oil producing company and the lynchpin of the Kingdom's economy. It is the major employer in the Eastern Province, and has always been headquartered in Dhahran. Its 43,500-strong workforce includes some 11,500 expatriates, a figure which is steadily being reduced as the Saudiisation programme takes effect. It is estimated that the oil and gas industries directly employ about one-fifth of the Eastern Province workforce.

Saudi Aramco divides its oil operations into two areas – the southern area is administered from Abqaiq, the major processing centre for crude oil and natural gas liquids (NGL); the northern area is administered from Ras Tannurah.

The Kuwait crisis led to Saudi Aramco's eagerness to increase the production capacity of the Eastern Province oil fields to ten million barrels per day. Large contracts were awarded for the opening up of the Hawiyyah field (part of the vast Ghawar configuration), the upgrading of onshore facilities in the Qatif and Marjan fields, the expansion offshore of the Marjan and Zuluf fields, and various pipeline and platform projects. The Ras Tannurah refinery

Exploration

Exploration for oil and gas proceeded throughout the 1970s and early 1980s, to establish as nearly as possible the extent of the country's phenomenal reserves. The search for reserves has since been resumed.

The presence of oil is first deduced, by aerial survey and ground investigation, from surface geological formations. Seismic tests follow and trial wells are then drilled, but making a commercial strike usually involves a lengthy process of trial and error. By 1985, fifty-nine commercial fields had been discovered, seventeen of them offshore, three partially so, and the rest onshore. The Ghawar field is the world's largest onshore field, producing 4.4 million barrels per day, and Safaniyyah the world's largest offshore, at 1.3 million barrels per day.

Geologists examine a seismographic cross-section.

was upgraded. At a projected cost of some $10-$15 billion, all this would represent an investment on a scale not seen since the construction of its Master Gas System between 1977 and 1982. Spending on this scale would bode well for the economic growth of the Eastern Province. Saudi Aramco has always been respected for its ability to carry out large projects at speed, and a construction boom was soon under way, helped along by SABIC's new projects at Jubail. The company's confidence that worldwide demand for its products would rise throughout the 1990s enabled it to borrow from banks to finance its expansion plans.

Today Saudi Aramco's policy also has a multinational thrust; it is diversifying downstream, taking control of profitable operations previously carried out by its customers and middlemen. It is investing in overseas refineries, marketing its own oil products abroad, and is in the process of commissioning its own tanker fleet.

Drilling and extraction

When a drilling rig strikes an underground reservoir, crude oil at first rises to the surface as a result of natural pressure exerted by the expansion of the dissolved gas which is trapped under pressure with the crude oil, and by water underlying the oil. The oil and associated gas then proceeds by flowlines to the Gas-Oil Separation Plant (GOSP). As the oil and gas are extracted, the reservoir pressure may drop, and it is then maintained by re-cycling back into the reservoir some of the gas from the GOSP, and injecting water from a seawater treatment plant such as the huge one at Qurayyah, south of Dhahran.

The unstabilised oil then proceeds to the crude oil stabiliser, which removes the toxic hydrogen sulphide from crude destined for export. From there it can be pumped through pipelines to its destination at Ras Tannurah or Ju'aymah oil terminals. Sour crude – unstabilised crude still with its hydrogen sulphide – can be piped direct to a refinery, where the hydrogen sulphide is removed as part of the refining process.

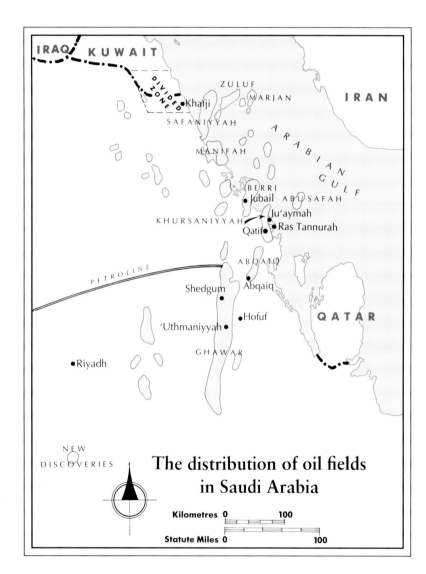

The distribution of oil fields in Saudi Arabia

An offshore rig and GOSP in the Safaniyyah field: crude oil is either loaded directly aboard tankers for export or piped to the mainland.

Drilling rods are stacked for use on a rig in the Safaniyyah field.

The advanced Arc 2000 drilling rig (*above*) probes below the deep Khuff gas zone in the 'Uthmaniyyah area. Drilling operations continue around the clock.

The first all-Saudi drilling crew, 1978 (*left*).

The Master Gas System

Until the mid-1970s oil production was accompanied by the wasteful and polluting flaring of much of the gas separated from the crude oil in the Gas-Oil Separation Plants. In the late 1970s and early 1980s, a massive engineering exercise was put in place to remedy this: the land-based Master Gas System, to collect all the gas separated off in the GOSPs. This involved adding large compression units to many GOSPs, which could then process the gas into natural gas liquids (NGL). Completed by 1982, in a remarkably short time and at a cost of some $12 billion, the system now sends raw gas and NGL to its various destinations, from major gas processing centres at Shedgum and 'Uthmaniyyah in the southern area, and Berri near Jubail in the northern area. Methane and ethane gas produced from NGL have now become the basic feedstock of several of the Eastern Province's large petrochemical enterprises, NGL is exported and some NGL with ethane is piped via Petroline to Yanbu on the Red Sea. Refined gas also fuels power stations and the sea water desalination plants at Jubail and al-Khobar.

Fin-fan coolers (*right*) stretch into the distance atop one of the two rebuilt fractionation modules at the Ju'aymah Gas Plant. The module's de-ethanizer column stands in the foreground.

GOSP in the Marjan field (*below*).

A Saudi Aramco employee (*right*) operates a distributed control system console at Abqaiq Plants.

Part of the Master Gas System.

Petroline

Conceived in the mid-1970s, the 1,200-kilometre Petroline began pumping oil and gas across Arabia from the Eastern Province to Yanbu on the Red Sea in the early 1980s. It is a strategically vital export alternative to the exposed tanker routes through the Gulf and Straits of Hormuz. It was used to its full capacity of 3.2 million barrels per day during the Kuwait crisis, and contracts are now being let to increase capacity to 4.8 million barrels per day. Petroline also saves a 4,960-kilometre voyage round the Peninsula to supply the growing refining and petrochemicals industry at Yanbu.

The 48-inch and 56-inch steel lines share eleven pumping stations from Abqaiq and 'Ayn Dar in the Eastern Province, to Yanbu, from where the entire line is controlled.

Piping refined products (*left*): a Saudi Aramco technician operates the valve.

These are the arteries of Saudi Arabia's oil industry (*left*). Petroleum pipes sweep out of Abqaiq Plants (*right*) at the start of the 1,200-kilometre East-West Crude Oil Pipeline to Yanbu in the Western Province.

Refining

There are two large refineries in the Eastern Province. The biggest, at Ras Tannurah, is owned by Saudi Aramco and is export-orientated, though its output was diverted to military use during the Kuwait crisis. Fuel oil accounts for about half the production of the Ras Tannurah refinery, which refines more than 530,000 barrels of crude oil daily. Its capacity is currently due to be increased, and plans are afoot to re-build parts of the refinery, some of which are now forty years old. The Jubail refinery is owned by Petromin-Shell and produces 250,000 bpd.

The heart of the oil refinery is the fractionating column of the crude oil distillation unit. Heated crude is fed into the bottom of the column, and is then flashed into vapours. Crude oil is

Ras Tannurah NGL plant (*above*) and the main refinery (*right*).

a mixture of different types of hydrocarbons, all having different boiling points. The vapours of the heavier hydrocarbons condense at a higher temperature near the bottom of the fractionating column. Those of the lighter hydrocarbons, such as kerosene and gasoline, bubble up through a series of trays until they condense at the relatively low temperature at the top. Thus, the process of distillation separates the crude oil into various "fractions". Each fraction in turn must be refined before it is ready for the market, as jet fuel, petrol, kerosene, naptha, fuel oil, diesel oil and asphalt.

Other plants at Ras Tannurah process stabilised NGL and fractionate it into three main components: butane, propane (both often called liquefied petroleum gas or LPG), and natural gasoline.

Export terminals

Ras Tannurah is one of the world's largest oil export terminals, with two piers and a sea island providing a total of eight loading berths. The loading capacity of the port is over 700,000 barrels per hour, and its storage tanks can hold up to 35 million barrels. Ju'aymah terminal is able to accommodate six tankers. There is a single loading buoy in the northern Gulf, at Zuluf. In addition, oil for export can be pumped across the Peninsula to Yanbu on the Red Sea via Petroline.

One of Saudi Aramco's fleet of tankers (*left*).

Ras Tannurah terminal, 1979 (*above*).

Research, administration and training

The entire process of exploration, drilling, separation, transport, refining and loading demands the most modern petroleum technology. Saudi Aramco runs its own administration and training schemes for employees, but the chief supplier of trained manpower to the oil industry is King Fahd University of Petroleum and Minerals in Dhahran. Today this is an internationally recognised centre of excellence which trains young Saudi Arabians to play their full part in the industry. Results have been good, and increasingly the industry is being operated and managed by Saudi Arabians, with 77 per cent of Saudi Aramco's supervisory posts and half of its professional posts held by the Kingdom's nationals.

Saudi Aramco's Exploration and Petroleum Engineering Center (EXPEC), Dhahran (*below*).

Saudi Aramco provides training facilities (*right*) for all its employees, with a full-time staff of 840 teachers, and 718 support personnel.

Researchers (*far right*) are currently developing 'clean fuels' to meet the increasing world demand for the reduction of atmospheric pollution.

Primary and secondary industries

SABIC and its partners

With its proximity to unlimited energy supplies and petrochemical feedstocks, the Eastern Province was the obvious choice for the location of major industries. The Kingdom's efforts to industrialise were, from the first, Government-led: they began in the 1970s, when the large state-owned Saudi Basic Industries Corporation (SABIC) was set up to enable the Kingdom to diversify downstream from crude oil exports and domestic refining.

The plan was to utilise Saudi Arabia's raw materials to turn it into a leading exporter of primary products (refined oil and gas products, basic petrochemicals, fertilisers) and secondary industries (value-added petrochemical products, plastics, agrochemicals, steel). SABIC's strategy was to form joint ventures with a number of leading international companies. It operated alongside the Royal Commission for Jubail and Yanbu, which was responsible for creating the two new industrial cities, to set up the first generation of petrochemical, fertiliser and steel plants. Most of these projects came on stream between 1983 and 1988, and most depend for power and feedstocks on the Master Gas System, which itself had come on stream as planned during the early 1980s.

SABIC companies flourished in the late 1980s, responding well to robust worldwide demand for petrochemical products. SABIC's total output rose from 8.5 million tonnes in 1987 to 12.1 million tonnes in 1990, by which time it already commanded a 5 per cent share of world petrochemical capacity to make it the Middle East's biggest producer.

SABIC has a sophisticated approach to marketing, selling its products to a wide spread of countries in North America, Europe and the Far East, and aiming to build up a direct, stable relationship with its customers. HADEED, for example, the Saudi Iron and Steel Company, has transformed the Kingdom from an importer to an exporter of steel products, with customers in Japan, Singapore, Taiwan and South Korea. New markets for SABIC products are opening up in Asia, Africa and the Middle East.

The private sector

Secondary industries, light manufacturing and services

The Government has for some time been encouraging private sector participation in SABIC enterprises. There are also signs that the private sector, assisted by SABIC expertise and minority shareholding, is throwing off its traditional reluctance to invest in large independent petrochemical enterprises. Already the Saudi Formaldehyde Chemical Company (SFCC) has come on stream at Jubail. Other Saudi industrial concerns and financial groups have projects under consideration, among them the Arabian Industrial Development Company (NAMA), which has been set up specifically to invest in projects in the Eastern Province, and the Saudi Venture Capital Group.

Traditional Eastern Province trading families – such as the al-Gosaibis, the al-Zamils, the al-Olayans and the Kanoos and others – have played a significant part in the development of the region. Local pipe-makers are expanding to meet orders, for example the National Pipe Company, based in al-Khobar. The al-Gosaibi family, which has a majority stake in the Saudi Steel Pipe Company, a joint venture with South Korean participation, is doubling the capacity of the business to

The Eastern Province has three cement plants including Saudi-Kuwaiti Cement (*above*).

Saudi Iron and Steel Company – HADEED – is a well-known Jubail landmark. Products for both the domestic and export markets include steel rods and wire coils.

take advantage of the expansion of the oil industry.

While Jubail is the domain of heavy primary and secondary industries, the smaller private sector secondary industries plus supporting and light manufacturing businesses have a much wider spread in the Province. Despite the attractions of Jubail for new small service businesses, factory start-ups are still overwhelmingly concentrated in Dammam's two large industrial estates, where over 170 factories operate. Building materials producers tend to set up as close to areas of raw materials as possible, and so are to be found in Hasa Oasis and Abqaiq as well as in Qatif. Generally speaking, however, Dammam is

favoured for manufacturing. Its products include industrial gases, chemicals, glass, asbestos, rubber products, building materials, paints, air conditioners, furniture, carpets, food, soft drinks and many more.

In a booming economy, service industries are quick to blossom. Local businessmen in the Eastern Province towns supply a wide range of services to industry and the public, from restaurants, hotels and supermarkets, to transport, cleaning, design, print, computers, film and photography, as well as a thriving banking sector. Well represented among the business names are those families with a long tradition of trade in the historic Eastern Province towns of Hofuf and Qatif.

Hand-crafted stained glass is produced in Dammam at Zamil Gibbs Art Glass. Many of the Kingdom's stunning decorative windows (e.g. the Saudi Aramco mosque at Dhahran) originate from here.

Full maintenance and support services are essential for helicopters operating in the oil industry.

Sealing agents which guard against damage from dust and water are manufactured by the al-Zamil group (*right*).

Rockbits (*left*), essential in a region dominated by drilling, are designed to bite through the earth's surface in the search for oil or water.

Safety valves for the oil industry are manufactured in Jubail (*right*).

Current primary industries at Jubail are predominantly hydrocarbon-based. One exception is HADEED's iron and steel mill (*right and below*) which uses large quantities of the energy readily available on site.

Quality control department at Al-Zamil Food Industries facilities in Jubail (*right*).

Jubail Industrial City

Today Jubail Industrial City – Madinat al-Jubail al-Sina'iyyah – exemplifies, with Yanbu on the Red Sea, the successful realisation of Saudi Arabia's commitment to diversified economic growth. It epitomises the Kingdom's determination to be master of its own industrial destiny.

Under a royal decree issued in 1975, the Royal Commission for Jubail and Yanbu was established and immediately set about fulfilling its brief: to provide the entire industrial and community infrastructure of the two cities.

The recently updated masterplan for Jubail covers 1,030 square kilometres. By 1991 the population had grown to 50,000, and plans were put in hand to increase provision for 60,000 people as industries expanded. The masterplan allows for growth by the year 2010 to 280,000 people, living in eight residential areas bounded by green, open space corridors. Each district will comprise several residential sections, each with a population of about 2,500, and each with its own mosques, elementary schools, shopping and recreational facilities.

The southern part of the city area is given over to Jubail's industries, while the northern part is the permanent community and residential area. Since the Jubail area is very flat, with salt marshes and unstable sand dunes, and not much above sea level, the entire site had to be raised from two to five metres above the marine flood threshold. At the same time this has reduced soil salinity and encouraged plant growth. This required the biggest earth-moving operation since the digging of the Panama Canal. It has been calculated that the quantity of earth moved during the construction of Jubail would be sufficient to girdle the globe with a road a metre deep and nine metres wide. Jubail, its landscape and its 45 kilometres of coastline, are essentially man-made.

The surroundings of Jubail are being stabilised by planting to prevent encroachment by sand and to reduce the dust nuisance to industrial installations. Much of this is experimental. The Royal Commission is anxious to minimise water consumption, and so is introducing a range of salt-tolerant plants which, it is hoped, will flourish and spread.

The new industries, under the aegis of SABIC, were all selected to make efficient use of the Eastern Province's petroleum

This aerial view of the old town of Jubail (*left*) was taken in 1933, the year the search for oil began. Today's Jubail Industrial City is located about 15km north of the old town and includes a residential area (*above*) planned to accommodate up to 280,000.

and other feedstocks, rapidly coming on stream with the creation of the Master Gas System which was completed in 1982. The economic heart of Jubail is the Primary Industries Park, which is planned to accommodate twenty large capital and energy-intensive industries. With the exception of

HADEED - the iron and steel mill - all of these industries use the Kingdom's hydrocarbon resources as feedstocks. Much of their output is for export, although increasing amounts are becoming the feedstocks for local downstream industries. Fifteen primary industry plants were in operation by the early 1990s, most of them joint ventures between SABIC and foreign companies or Saudi investors.

Principal downstream industries, their products aimed at import substitution and export, are located in the Secondary Industries Park, or within the primary area near a parent feedstock supplier. The task of the secondary industries is to upgrade primary industry products by further processing, thereby yielding petrochemical intermediates, such as plastic and steel products, and agricultural and other chemicals. Secondary industries include the Saudi Urethane Chemical Company,

manufacturing polyether polyols.

The Support and Light Manufacturing Industries Park contains smaller enterprises ranging from heavy commercial services such as industrial laundries to equipment dealerships offering goods and services needed by other industries and the Jubail community. Over 76 support and light industries are now operational.

From the start, the Royal Commission has believed education and development of the individual to be essential to the success of the industrialisation process, and priority was given to creating a comprehensive training institute at Jubail. Jubail's Industrial College (JIC) educates Saudi graduates in over 21 areas of expertise. Based upon the industrial, administrative and business needs of the city, courses now teach everything from process control technology to engineering skills and business administration.

Although Jubail is the flagship of the Kingdom's development plans, it is much more than its physical infrastructure and industrial complexes. It is a thriving residential community offering a high standard of living and intended to be a model of Islamic urbanisation. Its permanent housing in al-Fanateer and al-Deffi – started by the Royal Commission but today being built by industry, the private sector and individuals – provides a blend of modern architectural styles which is unmistakably Islamic. Jubail is a bold attempt to design a Saudi Arabian future which is unrelentingly modern, destined to be one of the foremost manufacturing centres of tomorrow's global marketplace, yet at the same time people-orientated – a community at one with traditional spiritual values.

The permanent residential community is situated to the north of the industrial area which can be seen in the background of the picture.

From the administrative headquarters of the Royal Commission (*above and right*) at Jubail, opened in 1983, every detail of the city's expansion is planned for and supervised.

Haii al-Fanateer (*left*) was the first of the eight residential areas to be developed at Jubail.

Private sector development is actively encouraged: the Holiday Inn (*below*) which was completed in 1986 is a highly successful example.

The Eastern Petrochemical Company (SHARQ) produces ethylene glycol and low-density polyethylene, used in the manufacture of plastic film.

Lit up at night Petromin-Shell's refinery at Jubail (*right*) makes a dramatic contribution to the skyline.

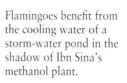

Flamingoes benefit from the cooling water of a storm-water pond in the shadow of Ibn Sina's methanol plant.

Jubail's King Fahd Industrial Port

Jubail's King Fahd Industrial Port is a triumph of construction. Occupying a ten-kilometre stretch of the coastline, it has twenty deep-water berths for dry and liquid bulk cargoes from Jubail's heavy industrial plants. To the south there is a smaller, separate commercial port for general cargo, built to serve the needs of the city's import/export markets for manufactured products and raw materials. The ports were built by the Royal Commission in cooperation with the Saudi Ports Authority.

Land reclamation dredging and coastal protection were necessary for the construction of port facilities.

Oil and petroleum related liquids are handled at Jubail's bulk liquid terminal (*left*).

At the end of a nine-kilometre causeway, King Fahd Industrial Port includes 20 deepwater berths.

King Fahd International Airport

Dhahran's old international airport, so familiar to the millions who passed through the region over the years, finally closed, the last flight taking off from the runway on 26 November 1999. In its place, and in time for the air traffic of the new Millennium, King Fahd International Airport was opened. With a site of 760 square kilometres on the coastal plain between Dhahran and Jubail, it is now the largest airport in the Kingdom. The first phase of opening included two brand new runways, a 200,000 square metre passenger terminal, eleven contact gates for loading, and a 4,000 square metre mosque. The new airport has been designed and constructed to handle up to 10 million passengers a year. Its buildings reflect Islamic architectural principles.

As well as serving the Dammam-Dhahran-al-Khobar and Qatif conurbations, the new airport is only a forty-minute drive from Jubail, where the existing domestic airport is being phased out.

Models of the new King Fahd International Airport and its Royal Pavilion (*above*). Meanwhile Saudia serves Dhahran.

Power generation

In the 1950s, electric power in the growing towns of the Eastern Province was provided by small local private companies, set up with Aramco's assistance. As demand for power increased it became necessary for a single large utility to control all supplies. After a series of mergers, Saudi Consolidated Electric Company (SCECO) was formed in 1976, with Aramco as manager for the first five years. SCECO was charged with supplying all the Eastern Province's industrial, commercial and domestic power requirements, and expanding the network as needed.

In the fifteen years between 1970 and 1985 generating capacity was increased twentyfold; it is planned to double again by the end of the century. Electricity costs to consumers are heavily subsidised by the Government. Demand rises every year. There are now plans to create an integrated electricity grid to link the Eastern Province and the Gulf states.

Sea water desalination plants are always associated with electricity generating plants, and the major complexes are situated at Khafji, Safaniyyah, Tanaqib, Jubail, Dammam, al-Khobar and 'Uqayr.

Line men carry out repairs on the power distribution network.

The Ghazlan Power Plant (*above, right*) is one of several contributing to SCECO's electricity grid which supplies the cities (Dammam, *right*) and industries of the Eastern Province.

Al-Khobar's Prince Saud
ibn Jiluwi Park
surrounded by the lights
of the city.

Qurayyah Power Plant.

Roads

A vigorous road-building programme has long been an infrastructural priority in the Eastern Province, where, as in the rest of the Kingdom, vast distances have to be covered to link it in to the nationwide network of highways.

Most recently, the government has concentrated on integrating Jubail Industrial City into the network, with the construction of a system of six-lane freeways, four-to-six lane expressways, feeder roads, local roads, and special module pathways for transporting loads of up to 2,500 tonnes.

King Fahd Causeway

The imposing King Fahd Causeway provides the first-ever land link between Saudi Arabia and Bahrain. A masterpiece of civil engineering, at 25 kilometres it is the longest causeway but one in the world. Built at a cost of $1.2 billion, it took four years to build and was opened in November 1986. The Causeway spans shallow sea with its five bridges, as well as stretches of reclaimed land, the largest being more of an artificial island, with a customs post and coastguard facilities. In 1990 it was used by a million vehicles carrying three million people.

Qarah Village, Al-Hasa (*top right*) and the oasis (*below*).

These pictures of the King Fahd Causeway, taken from the air at night, from the sea and by day, testify to its impressive engineering.

The railway today

The Dammam-Hofuf-Harad-Kharj-Riyadh railway was originally completed in 1951. A new, more direct line was installed in the 1980s which misses out Harad and Kharj. The railway continues to play an important part in the economic life of the Eastern Province. Its main business is freight, and its rolling stock today comprises 43 locomotives, 58 passenger coaches and 1,565 freight wagons.

The vital rail link between the country's capital and its principal Gulf port, Dammam, is run by the Saudi Railroad Organisation, established in 1966.

Water

Its naturally abundant ground-water resources in Hasa Oasis, Qatif and Tarut Island have been a fundamental factor throughout the Eastern Province's social and environmental evolution. In the modern era, however, it was recognised early that the growing need for industrial, agricultural and domestic water supplies could not be fulfilled by this non-renewable source without serious depletion.

One of the first responses, in the late 1960s and early 1970s, to this potential problem was to reorganise the entire Hasa Oasis irrigation system, to minimise water loss and improve drainage, so reducing the creeping salination of valuable agricultural land and making available more water for irrigation.

Soon after, the Government embarked upon a major programme of desalination of sea water. Today's desalination plant at Jubail is the largest in the world, producing 200 million gallons of fresh water per day. Much of this is piped to Riyadh, where it provides an astonishing eighty per cent of the capital's water supply. The re-mainder is used locally. Water for other Eastern Province consumption is supplied by the six other desalination plants along the coast.

The Fifth Five-Year Plan (1990-95) upholds the Government's resolve that water should be used responsibly, and notes that agriculture is still too dependent on the use of non-renewable water sources. Future demand is to be controlled, and more emphasis placed on reclaiming waste water for agricultural use.

The success of this policy will be closely linked to the Government's other agricul-

The role of public art – and of cascading water – is central to Dammam's town planning.

Water – throughout the centuries the most valued resource of the Eastern Province – feeds the oasis gardens of al-Hasa.

tural policies. Jubail has shown that it can succeed: the re-cycling of used water has already been common practice in Jubail for some years. Under the Royal Commission's direction, irrigation water for landscaping is obtained by reclaiming sanitary waste water; industrial waste water is reclaimed for industrial use and fire-fighting needs. In addition, the Royal Commission is currently conducting experiments with salt-tolerant plants which can be grown without the use of freshwater. In the future these plants may be exploitable as fodder.

Jubail Desalination Plant

The desalination plant at Jubail, the world's largest, takes water from the great seawater intake channel which also provides seawater cooling for Jubail's industrial plants. The flow of this vast system is calculated at some two-thirds of that of the Tigris and Euphrates Rivers combined. The Jubail desalination plant produces 200 million gallons of fresh water per day. The process produces some electricity, which is fed back into the plant.

Hasa Oasis irrigation scheme

The Government's project to re-organise and re-build the Hasa Oasis irrigation network in the late 1960s and early 1970s was, after the establishment of the government farms at Harad, one of the earliest large-scale agricultural projects in the Kingdom. Like Harad, its sheer scale gave it a profound social as well as agricultural impact.

The groundwater resources of the region are supplemented by the waters of the Gulf. Desalination plants like this one at Jubail produce 400 million cubic metres of fresh water per year; some of this is piped to Riyadh.

Qatif's natural springs (*above*) provide enough water to sport in. Dhahran goes one better with an Olympic pool (*right*).

Agriculture and food production

To the casual observer, perhaps the most astonishing aspect of Saudi Arabia's period of modernisation has been the transformation of this arid land into a major agricultural producer. The productivity even of such traditional strongholds of agriculture and gardening as Hasa and Qatif Oases has been greatly increased by Government investment and stimulus. More suprising has been the success of cereal-growing in apparently barren areas of desert.

The Government decided in the 1970s that it would make self-sufficiency in basic foods a national strategic aim, and commit resources to the welfare and development of its rural communities commensurate with its investment in urban areas.

The state has funded an entire rural infrastructure, including water resources projects such as dams and deep drilling, the re-organisation of Hasa Oasis irrigation, setting up training centres, and building a network of rural roads. Interest-free loans have been provided through the Saudi Arabian Agricultural Bank, and subsidies provided for up to half the cost of machinery, animal feed, seeds and fertilisers. Wheat has been bought at very favourable subvention prices by the Grain Silos and Flour Mills Organisation. A programme of free land distribution to farmers and agricultural companies was adopted. Agricultural support industries in both public and private sectors have been encouraged: in fertilisers, pesticides, meat processing, dairy produce, fruit and vegetable preservation and packing, and oil and fat manufacturing.

The results have been dramatic. Local fruit and vegetable production has boomed, and businessmen and investors have been attracted by the generous subsidies into desert areas. Notable successes have been the 115 poultry farms in Hasa Oasis, producing over 100 million eggs and three million chickens annually, its rice, sorghum and citrus crops, and the expansion of Hasa Oasis' fruit orchards and vegetable gardens.

The durability of the Saudi agricultural miracle will depend on the Government's ability to maintain the level of investment and subsidy, which will depend in turn on the wealth generated by the other sectors of the economy. It will also depend, crucially, on the maintenance of water sup-

Traditionally, the date palm grove has been synonymous with human settlement, and the basis of subsistence – as in Hofuf (*above*). Today they provide the background for thriving market gardening; and Harad wheat fields (*right*) exemplify the country's success as a major exporter of cereals.

Wheat irrigation

In statistical terms, wheat production is the Kingdom's most phenomenal success. Its policies of generous subsidies to wheat farmers, in 1984 running at no less than ten times the world price and currently running at about four times, have resulted in the original aim of self-sufficiency being far exceeded: from being an importer of wheat, the Kingdom grows, at almost four million tonnes per annum, more than four times its own annual requirement. Saudi Arabia is now the sixth largest wheat producer in the world and the largest in the Middle East, exporting to the Russian Federation and other countries, and sending wheat as food aid to needy Muslim countries such as Sudan and Bangladesh. The Government is now encouraging farmers to switch to other crops in which the Kingdom is not yet self-sufficient, particularly barley for animal feed. Its success will depend on judiciously pitching the level of subsidies for wheat and barley.

plies. Estimates of the ability of the Kingdom's underground aquifers to sustain the present rate of depletion vary widely: from twenty to two hundred years. However, the Government is anxious to reduce to the minimum non-sustainable use of this irreplaceable resource.

Dates

The Kingdom contains one-tenth of the world's mature, productive date palms. The palm gardens of Hasa and Qatif oases account for more than three million of these. Date farmers are assisted by the Ministry of Agriculture and Water's date and agricultural research centre outside Hofuf. Although dates are no longer a staple in the Saudi diet, they form an important supplementary part of it. Dates also form an important part of Saudi foreign aid programmes.

Dairy farming

Intensive dairy farming makes an important contribution to Saudi food production these days, using imported livestock. Saudi Arabia is almost completely self-sufficient in milk production and dairy products, produces half of its red meat, 65 per cent of its white meat requirement, and is an exporter of eggs.

Fisheries

Parts of the Eastern Province's Gulf coast, such as its mud-flats, sea-grass beds and coral reefs, form important nursery areas for fish and shrimp stocks. Much of this has now been disturbed by port and coastal developments. This, combined with as yet unquantified damage from oil pollution during the Kuwait crisis, has meant that Saudi Arabia's Gulf fisheries – small fleets based at Dammam and Darin on Tarut Island – have been limited. Favoured fishing grounds are off Dammam, Abu Ali and Manifah. The Government plans to embark on conservation measures to protect fish stocks and breeding grounds.

Fish farms – like that above, established with advice from Saudi Aramco – breed tilapia, which is rich in protein. The Gulf itself teems with excellent fish to be purchased in Dammam's fish market (*below*).

The unbeatable quality of goats – traditional source of milk and meat – is their hardihood, as with this flourishing herd at al-Hasa. By contrast, cows (*top*) need constant shade and special feeds, though their yield is greater.

The environment

The years of rapid development and changes to the inland and coastal landscapes of the Eastern Province have brought with them a growing awareness of environmental issues, at both the public and governmental levels. The Kuwait oil spill crisis of January-February 1991 served to bring the environment to the forefront of public concern, and has firmly fixed it at the centre of policy-making.

Urbanisation, industrial growth and the creation of a transport infrastructure have consumed enormous tracts of land and stretches of coast. With the exception of Hasa and Qatif Oases, these used to be viewed largely as worthless desert. Today one is more likely to encounter the view that the land and marine environments of the Eastern Province include fragile ecosystems which must be protected. Many species are living at the limits of tolerance – a fact which increases their importance and interest. Such awareness now permeates all government organisations working in the Eastern Province, none more so than the Royal Commission for Jubail and Yanbu, whose urban planning and environmental improvement schemes at Jubail are widely admired.

Specialist national bodies are also at work: the Meteorological and Environmental Protection Agency (MEPA), and the National Commission for Wildlife Development and Conservation (NCWDC). The NCWDC is responsible for designating and managing the Kingdom's nature reserves. Reserves in the Eastern Province are planned to cover large tracts of land in the Empty Quarter, and an area stretching from Hasa Oasis to the coast, south of Half Moon Bay. Such reserves are not new in Arabia: they are merely a modern application of the concept of the *hima* or protected area, which dates from pre-Islamic times. The environmental stresses of modern times have given a new relevance to the idea of the *hima*.

The NCWDC's plans reflect the store set by the Eastern Province's coast and islands. The coastal and marine habitats include sandy and rocky beaches, tidal flats, seagrass beds, coral reefs and low coral islands. Warmth, shallowness and high salinity are the chief characteristics of the Arabian side of the Gulf. As well as a varied fish population, green and hawksbill turtles, porpoises and dugongs inhabit this fragile environment. The Arabian coast forms an important part of a major bird migration route between north and south.

The NCWDC's most advanced project is the designation as reserves of the coral islands – including Jinnah, Jana, Karan, Harqus and Juraid – with their rich turtle and tern nesting areas. The Gulf of Salwah, the area around Ras al-Qurayyah, Tarut Bay with its nutrient-rich mud flats and seagrass beds, Abu Ali and Ras al-Zawr, and Safaniyyah with Manifah Bay – all these are to be zoned as protected areas. The northernmost ones were severely damaged by the Kuwait oil spill, and it remains to be seen how far they can be revived.

Caspian terns flock to their nesting sites on the sanctuary of Karan island, north of Jubail. The survival of the rare Houbara bustard (*above*) has been assured by the National Commission for Wildlife Conservation and Development.

While unable to compete with the coral reefs of the country's western Red Sea waters, the Gulf inshore waters have their own coral and sea-grass wonders to display to the diver.

Abqaiq's Green Belt project (*below*) maintains the frontier of the sand desert.

Now that the green turtle is a protected species, its chief enemy is no longer man the hunter but man the sea-polluter.

The Kuwait oil pollution crisis

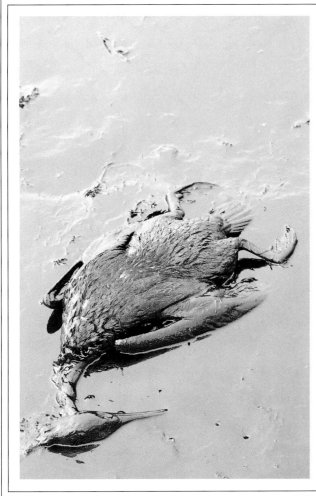

For a time it seemed as if the occupation of Kuwait, the firing of its oil wells, and the deliberate release of oil into the Gulf, had devastated the region's environment. The skies over the Eastern Province were darkened, and there were fears that hardened and emulsified oil would blanket large areas of the Gulf sea bed. The world over, television news programmes broadcast the plight of the many oiled sea birds struggling for life.

The first oil slick, caused by an Iraqi missile hitting a storage tank at Khafji in the Divided Zone, appeared in the northern Gulf at the end of January 1991. A major catastrophe in its own right, at as much as one million barrels, it was the biggest Gulf spill since the Nowruz disaster of 1983 during the Iran-Iraq War. Shortly afterwards a larger one began to appear, further out to sea in the Gulf. Variously estimated at the time at between five and eleven million barrels, this was to be the world's biggest marine oil pollution disaster, outdoing the previous record of 3.3 million barrels spilled into the Gulf of Mexico in 1979. It was started by the deliberate opening of the valves at Kuwait's oil port, Mina al-Ahmadi, and the emptying of tankers moored there. When US bombers managed to reduce this flow to a trickle, a third slick was deliberately started from Mina al-Bakr in Iraq.

The combined total of oil released during the war into the waters of the Gulf by Iraqi and allied action is now thought to stand at around six million barrels. Since the currents in the Gulf circle in an anti-clockwise direction, the coast most threatened by this killing tide was that of the Eastern Province mainland and islands. Helped by northerly winds, the oil came ashore along the 460-kilometre coastline north of Abu Ali – the richest mangrove swamps, intertidal flats, salt marshes and coral reefs, almost all of which have been severely damaged, many irrevocably.

First victims of the 1991 assault by oil were marine birds.

Traditional dhows are still in use today.

The clean-up operation

Defence against the oil slicks was approached in three stages. Most urgent was emergency protection for essential facilities, particularly the industrial installations at Jubail and the sea-water intakes for the desalination plants at Khafji, Safaniyyah, Tanaqib and Jubail. Next came the containment of the oil and its recovery into ships and trucks. Third came the clean-up process, a long task which still continues wherever fouling remains.

MEPA, Saudi Aramco, Petromin, The Royal Commission for Jubail and Yanbu and the NCWDC played vital roles in the clean-up operation, and they were assisted by an international effort. Floating booms, skimmers to suck up the oil, and storage tanks were flown in. Saudi Aramco had several oil-recovery vessels in operation. Experts arrived from all over the world. By mid-February oil was being recovered from the sea at a rate of 30,000 barrels per day, most to be stored on land, while a small proportion was added to the refining process at Jubail. International public opinion, already outraged by the atrocities against the people of Kuwait, was further aroused by the wanton use of the environmental weapon. The Jubail Wildlife Rescue Centre was set up by the NCWDC in cooperation with the Royal Commission for Jubail and Yanbu. The NCWDC coordinated international organisations such as the UK's RSPCA, the many outside experts, and the volunteers who brought in oiled birds and helped with the cleaning and care of stricken birds and turtles.

It is still too soon to judge how far the clean-up operation was successful. One can say that, as with the atmospheric pollution from the burning oil wells of Kuwait, the prophets of ecological doom have not been vindicated. It is, however, entirely probable that the northern Gulf environment may never recover fully from the world's worst-ever act of environmental terrorism.

Teams from Saudi Aramco and the Royal Commission led the operation to rescue the environment from the oil spill. The area around the more northerly desalination plants at Khafji and Safaniyyah (*left*) came under immediate threat.

Prospects for the environment

Since the discovery of oil, the Eastern Province environment has had much to endure: industrial and urban development, the creation of a modern infrastructure, an agricultural revolution, over-grazing and over-hunting, and the sudden additional stresses of war and environmental terrorism on a grand scale. As an ecologically marginal region, in which most species were already surviving at the limits of their tolerance, it has become a globally significant laboratory for the study of the impact of the modern world upon arid regions.

Yet there is much hope for the future. The events of 1990 and 1991 have given environmental issues a platform hitherto denied them. Researchers have flocked to the Eastern Province from all over the world, and there is already a new understanding not only of the fragility but of the complexity and value of the Gulf's ecosystems. Above all, there is a new feeling that the environment cannot be taken for granted.

This sense that man is a part of the environment, that it is vital to man's well-being, and that if he destroys it he destroys himself, is nothing new. Yet there is now a more acute awareness that man has the power to make or unmake the biosphere which supports all life. The Qur'an teaches that man may make use of nature for his own benefit, but also that man has a duty to care for it and nurture it. This concept of stewardship extends beyond that of enlightened self-interest to include the notion of man as trustee, with responsibility to ensure that nature is truly respected as part of God's creation, and that it is not impoverished for future generations.

A Historical Bibliography of The Eastern Province

Abbreviations

Atlal *Atlal – The Journal of Saudi Arabian Archaeology.* Riyadh.

BTAA *Bahrain Through the Ages – The Archaeology,* ed. Shaikha Haya Al Khalifa and Michael Rice, London, 1986.

EI² *The Encyclopaedia of Islam* second edition, Leiden and London 1960-86, in progress.

GJ *The Geographical Journal.* London.

PSAS *Proceedings of the Seminar for Arabian Studies.* London.

ABU DURUK, H. On Thumamah in "News and Events", *Atlal* 7, 1983. "The Excavation of a Neolithic Site at Thumama", *Atlal* 8, Riyadh, 1984.

ABU EZZAH, A. "The Political Situation in Eastern Arabia at the Advent of Islam", *PSAS* 9, 1979.

ABU HAKIMA, A. *History of Eastern Arabia, 1750-1800 – the Rise and Development of Bahrain and Kuwait.* London, 1965. *The Modern History of Kuwait, 1750-1965.* London, 1983.

ADAMS, R., P. PARR, M. IBRAHIM and A. AL-MUGHANNUM "Saudi Arabian Archaeological Reconnaissance – 1976. Preliminary Report on the First Phase of the Comprehensive Archaeological Survey Program", *Atlal* 1, 1977.

AL-ANSARY, 'ABD AL-RAHMAN *Qaryat al-Faw – a Portrait of a Pre-Islamic Civilisation in Saudi Arabia.* London, 1982.

ARAMCO. *ARAMCO World Magazine.* May-June, 1984.

ARMSTRONG, H.C. *Lord of Arabia. Ibn Saud – An Intimate Study of a King.* London, 1934.

AL-BALADHURI *The Origins of the Islamic State. The Futuh al-Buldan* of al-Baladhuri tr. P.K. Hitti. London and New York, 1916.

BASSON, P.W., J.BURCHARD, J. HARDY and A. PRICE *Biotopes of the Western Arabian Gulf.* ARAMCO, Dhahran, 1978.

BEESTON, A.F.L. "Hadjar", *EI²,* 1971. "Functional Significance of the Old South Arabian Town", *PSAS,* 1971. "The Hasaean Tombstone J 1052", *JANES* 11, 1979.

BIBBY, G. *Looking for Dilmun.* New York, 1969. *Preliminary Survey in Eastern Arabia, 1968.* Aarhus, 1973.

BOUCHARLAT, R. and J-F. SALLES "The History and Archaeology of the Gulf from the 5th Century BC to the 7th Century AD: a Review of the Evidence", *PSAS* 11, 1981.

BOWEN, R. LEBARON. "The Early Arabian Necropolis of 'Ain Jawan", *Bulletin of the American Schools of Oriental Research* Supplementary Studies nos.7-9, 1950.

BOXER, C.R. *The Portuguese Seaborne Empire, 1415-1825.* London, 1969.

BULLIET, R.W. *The Camel and the Wheel.* Cambridge, Mass., 1975.

BUNDY, G., R.J.CONNOR and C.J.O HARRISON *Birds of the Eastern Province of Saudi Arabia.* London and Dhahran, 1989.

BURCKHOLDER, G. "Steatite carvings from Saudi Arabia", *Artibus Asiae* 33, 1971. "Ubaid Sites and Pottery in Saudi Arabia", *Archaeology* 25, 1972.

CAETANI, L. *Annali dell' Islam,* vols. 1 and 2. Milan, 1905-7.

CANARD, M. "Al-Djannabi", *EI²,* 1965.

CASKEL, W. "Eine unbekannte Dynastie in Arabia", *Oriens* 2 [On the Jabrids of al-Hasa], 1949. " 'Abd al-Kais", *EI²,* 1960. " 'Amir b. Sa' sa' a' ", *EI²,* 1960. "Bakr b. Wa'il", *EI²,* 1960.

CHAPMAN, R.W. "Climatic Changes and the Evolution of Land Form in the Eastern Province of Saudi Arabia", *Geological Society of America Bulletin* 82, 1971.

CHEESMAN, R.E. "The Deserts of Jafurah and Jabrin", *GJ* 65, 1925. *In Unknown Arabia.* London, 1926.

CLEUZIOU, S. "Three Seasons at Hili: Towards a Chronology and Cultural History of the Oman Peninsula in the 3rd Millennium BC", *PSAS* 10, 1980. "Hili and the Beginning of Oasis Life in Eastern Arabia", *PSAS* 12, 1982.

COLE, D.P. *Nomads of the Nomads – the Al Murrah Bedouin of the Empty Quarter.* Arlington Heights, Illinois, 1975.

CORNWALL, P.B. "Ancient Arabia: Explorations in Hasa – 1940-41", *GJ* 107, Jan.-Feb., 1946. "Two Letters from Dilmun", *Journal of Cuneiform Studies* 6, 1952.

CORTESAO, A. and A.T. DA MOTA. *Monumenta Cartographica Portugaliae.* Lisbon, 1960-3.

COTTRELL, A.J. ed. *The Persian Gulf States.* Johns Hopkins U.P., 1980.

CRARY, D.D. "Recent Agricultural Developments in Saudi Arabia". New York. *Geographical Review* 41, 1951.

AL-DAKHIL, SULAIMAN *Ta'rikh al-'Ahsa.* 1331 AH.

DAME, L.P. "Four Months in Nejd", *The Moslem World* 14, 1924.

DE BLOIS, F. "The Abu Sa'idis or so-called 'Qarmatians' of Bahrayn", *PSAS* 16, 1986.

DE GOEJE, M.J. *Mémoire sur les Carmathes du Bahrain.* Leiden. 1886. "La fin de l'empire des Carmathes du Bahrain", *Journal Asiatique* Series 9, 5, 1895.

DEPARTMENT OF ANTIQUITIES AND MUSEUMS, RIYADH. *An Introduction to Saudi Arabian Antiquities.* Riyadh, 1975.

DI MEGLIO, R. "Banu Khalid", *EI²,* 1978.

DICKSON, H.R.P. *The Arab of the Desert.* London, 1949. *Kuwait and Her Neighbours.* London, 1956.

DICKSON, H.R.P. and V.P. "Thaj and Other Sites", *Iraq* 10, 1948.

DONNER, F. McG. "The Bakr b. Wa'il Tribes and Politics in Northeastern Arabia on the Eve of Islam", *Studia Islamica* 51, 1980. *The Early Islamic Conquests.* Princeton, 1981.

DOSTAL, W. "The Evolution of Bedouin Life", *L'Antica Societa Bedouina,* ed. Gabrielli. Rome, 1959.

DOWSON, V.H.W. "The Date and the Arab", *Journal of the Royal Central Asian Society* 36, 1949.

DURING CASPERS, E.C.L. "Corals, Pearls and Prehistoric Gulf Trade", *PSAS* 13, 1983.

EBERT, C.H.V. "Water Resources and Land Use in the Qatif Oasis of Saudi Arabia", *Geographical Review* 55 (iv), 1965.

ESKOUBI, K.M. and S.R. ABU AL-ULA "Thaj Excavations, Second Season", *Atlal* 9, 1985.

FACEY, W.H.D. *Oman – A Seafaring Nation.* Muscat, 1979. "The Boat Carvings at Jabal al-Jussasiyyah, Northeast Qatar", *PSAS* 17, 1987. *Riyadh – The Old City.* London, 1992.

FLOOR, W.M. "A Description of the Persian Gulf and its Inhabitants in 1756", *Persica* 8, 1979.

FROHLICH, B. and A. MUGHANNUM "Excavation of the Dhahran Burial Mounds, 1984", *Atlal* 9, 1985.

FRYE, R.N. "Bahrain Under the Sasanians", in *Dilmun* ed. Potts. Berlin, 1983.

GAZDAR, M.S., D.T. POTTS and A. LIVINGSTONE "Excavations at Thaj", *Atlal* 8. Includes "A Linguistic, Tribal and Onomastical Study of the Hasaean Inscriptions", 1984.

GLASSÉ, C. *The Concise Encyclopaedia of Islam.* Stacey International, London, 1989.

GOLDING, M. "Artefacts from Later Pre-Islamic Occupation in Eastern Arabia", *Atlal* 8, 1984.

GREAT BRITAIN, HYDROGRAPHIC DEPT., ADMIRALTY *Persian Gulf Pilot.* London, 1967.

GREAT BRITAIN, ADMIRALTY WAR STAFF, INTELLIGENCE DIVISION *A Handbook of Arabia.* London, 1916.

GREAT BRITAIN, ADMIRALTY, NAVAL INTELLIGENCE DIVISION. *Iraq and the Persian Gulf.* London, 1944.

GROHMANN, A. "Al-'Arab", *EI²,* 1960.

GROOM, N. ST.J. *Frankincense and Myrrh.* Harlow, 1981. "Gerrha – a 'Lost' Arabian City", *Atlal* 6, 1982. "Eastern Arabia in Ptolemy's Map", *PSAS* 16, 1986.

HAARMANN, U. "Murtada b. 'Ali b. 'Alawan's Journey Through Arabia in 1121/1709", in *Sources for the History of Arabia.* Riyadh, 1979.

HABIB, J.S. *Ibn Sa'ud's Warriors of Islam: the Ikhwan of Najd and their Role in the Creation of the Sa'udi Kingdom 1910-1930.* Leiden, 1978.

HARRISON, P.W. *The Arab at Home.* London, 1924.

HEARD-BEY, F. *From Trucial States to United Arab Emirates.* Harlow, 1982.

HENDERSON, E.F. "Tribal Organisation in Eastern Arabia in the Islamic Era", *PSAS* 12, 1982.

HOGARTH, D.G. *The Penetration of Arabia.* London, 1904. "Some Recent Arabian Explorations", *The Geographical Review* vol. XI no.3, July, 1921.

HOLDEN, D. and R. JOHNS *The House of Saud.* London, 1982.

HOWARTH, D. *The Desert King. A Life of Ibn Saud.* London, 1964.

IBN BATTUTAH *Voyages d'Ibn Batoutah.* Arabic text with translation into French by C. Defrémery and B. Sanguinetti. Paris, 1854. *The Travels of Ibn Battuta A.D. 1325-1354.* Translated, edited and annotated, from the text of Defrémery and Sanguinetti, by H.A.R. Gibb, Hakluyt Society, Cambridge, 1958.

IPPOLITINI-STRIKA, F. "The Tarut Statue as a Peripheral Contribution to the Knowledge of Early Mesopotamian Plastic Art", *BTAA,* 1983.

JADO, A. and J. ZÖTL *Quaternary Period in Saudi Arabia,* vol.2. Vienna and New York, 1984.

JAMES, W.E. "On the Location of Gerrha", in *Die Araber in der alten Welt* vol.5 ii. Berlin, 1969.

JAMME, A. *Sabaean and Hasaean Inscriptions from Saudi Arabia.* Studi Semitici 23, Rome, 1966. "New Hasaean and Sabaean Inscriptions from Saudi Arabia", *Oriens Antiquus* 6, 1967.

AL-JUHANY, U.M. *The History of Najd prior to the Wahhabis; a Study of Social, Political and Religious Conditions in Najd during Three Centuries Preceding the Wahhabi Reform Movement.* Ann Arbor, 1983.

KELLY, J.B. *Eastern Arabian Frontiers.* London, 1964. "Mehemet Ali's Expedition to the Persian Gulf 1837-1840, Part 1", *Middle Eastern Studies* vol.1, no.4, July, 1965. Ditto, Part 2, *Middle Eastern Studies* vol.2, no.1, Oct., 1965. *Britain and the Persian Gulf.* Oxford, 1968. *Arabia, the Gulf and the West.* London.

KEMBALL, A.B. "Memoranda on the Resources, Localities and Relations of the Tribes Inhabiting the Arabian Shores of the Persian Gulf." *Bombay Selections* vol. 24, Jan., pp.111-114. Quotes Lt. Jopp's route in Nov. 1841 from Ojair to al-Hofuf. 1845.

KING, G. "Islamic Architecture in Eastern Arabia", *PSAS* 8, 1978. *The Historical Mosques of Saudi Arabia.* London, 1986.

LACEY, R. *The Kingdom.* London, 1981.

LARSEN, C.E. "The Early Environment and Hydrology of Ancient Bahrain", in *Dilmun* ed. D.T. Potts. Berlin, 1983.

LASSNER, J. "Kays", *EI²,* 1978.

LEACHMAN, G. "A Journey through Central Arabia", *GJ* 43. 1915.

LEBKICHER, R., G.RENTZ and M.STEINEKE *The Arabia of Ibn Saud.* New York, 1952

LOCKHART, L. "Hurmuz", *EI²,* 1971.

LORIMER, J.G. *Gazetteer of the Persian Gulf, Oman and Central Arabia.* 2 vols. Calcutta, 1908-15.

LYALL, C.J. *Translations of Ancient Arabian Poetry, Chiefly Prae-Islamic.* London, 1885.

MACKIE, J.B. "Hasa: an Arabian Oasis", *GJ* 53, March, 1924.

MADELUNG, W. "Karmati", *EI²,* 1978.

MANDAVILLE, J.E. "The Ottoman Province of al-Hasa in the Sixteenth and Seventeenth Centuries", *Journal of the American Oriental Society* 90, 1970. *Al-Ahsa in the Islamic Period.* Unpublished paper produced for Local Museums research project, Department of Antiquities and Museums, Riyadh, 1984.

MANDAVILLE, J.P. "Thaj – a Pre-Islamic

Site in Northeast Arabia", *Bulletin of the American Schools of Oriental Research* 172, 1963. *Flora of Eastern Saudi Arabia*. London, 1990.

MASRY, A.H. *Prehistory in Northeastern Arabia: the Problem of Interregional Interaction*. Miami, 1974.

MUGHANNUM, A. "Sasanid Dirhams from the island of Tarut", *BTAA* – Volume 2, the History. London, forthcoming.

MULLIGAN, W.E. " 'Awazim", *EI²*, 1960.

NAWWAB, I.I. *ARAMCO and its World*. Washington D.C., 1980.

NICHOLSON, E. *In the Footsteps of the Camel. A Portrait of the Bedouins of Eastern Arabia in Mid-Century*. Riyadh/ London, 1983.

NIEBUHR, C. *Description de l'Arabie*. Amsterdam, 1774.

NISSEN, H.J. "The Occurrence of Dilmun in the Oldest Texts of Mesopotamia", *BTAA*, 1983.

NORBERG, C. *Gihan Numa* of Hajji Khalifah, tr. into Latin and ed. Norberg. Gotha, 1818 (Reprinted 1973).

OATES, D. "Dilmun and the Late Assyrian Empire", *BTAA*, 1983.

OATES, D. and J. *The Rise of Civilisation*. Oxford, 1976.

OATES, J. "Prehistory in Northeastern Arabia", *Antiquity* 50, 1976. "Ubaid Mesopotamia and its Relation to Gulf Countries", in *Qatar Archaeological Report, Excavations 1973*, ed. B. de Cardi. Oxford, 1978.

OATES, J., D. KAMILLI and H. McKERRELL "Seafaring Merchants of Ur?", *Antiquity* 51, 1977.

OZBARAN, S. "The Ottoman Turks and the Portuguese in the Persian Gulf, 1534-1581", *Journal of Asian History* 6, 1972.

PALGRAVE, W.G. "Notes of a Journey from Gaza, through the Interior of Arabia, to El Khatif on the Persian Gulf, and thence to Oman, in 1862-3", *Proceedings of the Royal Geographical Society* vol.VIII, 1863-4. "Observations Made in Central, Eastern and Southern Arabia during a Journey through that Country in 1862 and 1863", *Journal of the Royal Geographical Society* vol.XXXIV, 1864. *Narrative of a Year's Journey Through Central and Eastern Arabia (1862-3)*. 2 vols., London, 1865. *Personal Narrative of a Year's Journey Through Central and Eastern Arabia*, new (abridged) edition, in one volume. London, 1868.

PARR, P.J. "Objects from Thaj in the British Museum", *Bulletin of the American Schools of Oriental Research* 176, 1964.

PELLY, L. "Remarks on the Tribes, Trade and Resources around the Shore Line of the Persian Gulf", *Transactions of the Bombay Geographical Society* 17, 1863. "Visit to the Wahabee Capital of Central Arabia", *Proceedings of the Royal Geographical Society* 9, 1864-5. "A visit to the Wahabee Capital, Central Arabia", *Journal of the Royal Geographical Society* 35, 1865. *Report on a Journey to Riyadh in Central Arabia, 1865*. Bombay, 1866 (reprinted Cambridge 1978).

PHILBY, H.ST.J.B. "Across Arabia: from the Persian Gulf to the Red Sea",

Journal of the Royal Geographical Society 56, 1920. *The Heart of Arabia*. 2 vols., London, 1922. *Arabia of the Wahhabis*. London, 1928. *The Empty Quarter*. London, 1933. *Sa'udi Arabia*. London, 1955.

PHILIPP, H.-J. *Geschichte und Entwicklung der Oase al-Hasa (Saudi Arabien)*. Saarbrücken, 1976.

PIACENTINI, V.F. "Ardashir I Papakan and the wars against the Arabs: working hypothesis on the Sasanian hold of the Gulf", *PSAS* 15, 1985.

POTTS, D.T., A.S. MUGHANNUM, J.FRYE and D SANDERS "Preliminary Report on the Second Phase of the Eastern Province Survey, 1397/1977", *Atlal* 2, 1978.

POTTS, D.T., ed. *Dilmun – New Studies in the Archaeology and Early History of Bahrain*. Berlin, 1983.

POTTS, D.T. "Thaj in the Light of Recent Research", *Atlal* 7, 1983. "Dilmun: Where and When", *Dilmun* 11, 1983. "Northeastern Arabia in the Late Pre-Islamic Era", *Arabie orientale, Mésopotamie et Iran méridional de l'Age du Fer au début de la période islamique*, ed. R. Boucharlat and J.-F. Salles. Paris, 1984. "Thaj and the Location of Gerrha", *PSAS* 14, 1984. "Northeastern Arabia under the Sasanians, Lakhmids and Early Caliphs", *Studies in the Archaeology and Early History of Northeastern Arabia*. "Nippur and Dilmun in the 14th Century BC", *PSAS* 16, 1986. *The Arabian Gulf in Antiquity*. Volume 1; *From Prehistory to the Fall of the Achaemenid Empire*. Volume 2; *From Alexander the Great to the Coming of Islam*. Oxford, 1990.

AL-RASHID, Z.M. *Sa'udi Relations with Eastern Arabia and 'Uman (1800-1871)*. London, 1981.

RAUNKIAER, B. *Through Wahhabiland on Camel-back*. London, 1969.

RENDEL, GERALDINE "Across Saudi Arabia", *Geographical Magazine* 6, 1938.

RENTZ, G. "Pearling in the Persian Gulf", *Semitic and Oriental Studies Presented to W. Popper*. Berkeley, 1951. "Djazirat al-'Arab", *EI²*, 1965. "Al-Dawasir", *EI²*, 1965. "Al-Ikhwan", *EI²*, 1971. "Wahhabism and Saudi Arabia", in *The Arabian Peninsula – Society and Politics*, ed. Hopwood. London, 1972. "Al-Katif", *EI²*, 1978. "Khadir, Banu", *EI²*, 1978.

RENTZ, G. and J.MANDAVILLE "Banu Hadjir", *EI²*, 1971.

RENTZ, G. and W.E.MULLIGAN "Al-Bahrayn", *EI²*, 1960.

RICE, M. *Dilmun Discovered*. London, 1983. *Search for the Paradise Land*. London, 1984.

RIHANI, A. *Ibn Sa'oud of Arabia. His People and His Land*. London, 1928. *Around the Coasts of Arabia*. London, 1930.

RYCKMANS, J. "A Three Generations' Matrilineal Genealogy in a Hasaean Inscription: Matrilineal Ancestry in Pre-Islamic Arabia", *BTAA*, 1983.

SADLEIR, G.F. "Account of a Journey from Katif on the Persian Gulf to Yamboo on the Red Sea...", *Transactions of the Literary Society of Bombay III*, 1923. *Diary of a Journey across Arabia (1819)*. Bombay, 1966 (reprinted with an Introduction by

F.M. Edwards, Cambridge 1977).

SAUDI ENGINEERING CONSULTANTS BUREAU (SECON) Vol.1: *General Report on the History of al-Hasa and its Historic Forts and Fortifications*. Vol.2: *Qasr Ibrahim*. Vol.3: *Qasr Sahud*. Vol.4: *Qasr Khezam*. Conservation report and masterplan prepared for Department of Antiquities and Museums, Riyadh, 1983.

SAYARI, S. and J.ZÖTL. *The Quaternary Period in Saudi Arabia: Central and Eastern Saudi Arabia*. Vienna and New York, 1978.

SCHEFER, C. *Sefer Nameh – Relation du voyage de Nassiri Khosrau*. Amsterdam, 1970.

SERJEANT, R.B. "Historical Sketch of the Gulf in the Islamic Era from the 7th to the 18th Century AD", *Qatar Archaeological Report, Excavations 1973*, ed. B. de Cardi. Oxford, 1978.

SHOUFANI, E.S. *Al-Riddah and the Muslim Conquest of Arabia*. Toronto, 1972.

SMITHERS, R. *Bedouin Development in Saudi Arabia: the Haradh Project*. Ford Foundation, Beirut, 1966.

STACEY INTERNATIONAL *The Kingdom of Saudi Arabia*. London, 1990.

STEGNER, W. *Discovery! The Search for Arabian Oil*. Beirut, 1971.

STEVENS, J.H. "Oasis Agriculture in the Central and Eastern Arabian Peninsula", *Geography* 57, 1972. "Man and Environment in Eastern Saudi Arabia", *Arabian Studies I*, 1974.

TEIXEIRA, PEDRO *The Travels of Pedro Teixeira; with his "Kings of Harmuz"* ... Tr. and ed. W. Sinclair. Hakluyt Society, London, 1967.

THOMAS, H., S.SEN, M.KHAN ET AL "The Lower Miocene Fauna of Al-Sarrar (Eastern Province, Saudi Arabia)", *Atlal* 5, 1981.

THOMAS, R.H. ed. *Arabian Gulf Intelligence: Selections from the Records of the Bombay Government*, New Series, no.XXIV, 1856. Bombay, 1985 [re-printed Cambridge 1985].

TOSI, M. "The Emerging Picture of Prehistoric Arabia", *Annual Review of Anthropology* 15, 1986. "Early Maritime Cultures of the Arabian Gulf and Indian Ocean", *BTAA*, 1986.

TROELLER, G. *The Birth of Saudi Arabia*. London, 1976.

TUETEY, C.G. *Classical Arabic Poetry: 162 Poems from Imrulkais to Ma'arri*. London, 1985.

TUSON, P. *The Records of the British Residency and Agencies in the Persian Gulf*. India Office Library and Records, London, 1979. "Lieutenant Wyburd's Journal of an Excursion into Arabia", *Arabian Studies* 5, 1979.

TWITCHELL, K.S. "Water Resources of Saudi Arabia", *Geographical Review* 34, 1944. *Saudi Arabia. With an Account of the Development of its Natural Resources*. 2nd edition. Princeton, 1953.

UHLIG, D. "Das Be-und Entwasserorungs Projekt de Al Hassa Oasen in Saudi Arabia", *Wasserwirtschaft* 55 (2), 1965.

VIDAL, F.S. "Date Culture in the Oasis of al-Hasa' ", *Middle East Journal* 8, 1954. *The Oasis of al-Hasa*. Dhahran, 1955. "Al-Hasa", *EI²*, 1971. "Al-Hufuf", *EI²*, 1971. "Development of

the Eastern Province: a Case Study of Al-Hasa Oasis", in *King Faisal and the Modernisation of Saudi Arabia*, ed. W.A. Beling, London, 1980.

VON OPPENHEIM, M. *Die Bedouinen*, 1952.

WEBSTER, R. "Camels in the Mythology of the Bedouin of the Rub' al-Khali", *Al-Ma'thurat al-Sha'biyyah*, no. 17, Qatar, Jan. 1990.

WHITCOMB, D. "The Archaeology of al-Hasa Oasis in the Islamic Period", *Atlal* 2, 1978.

WHITEHOUSE, D. "Sasanian Maritime Expansion", paper delivered at the Indian Ocean in Antiquity Conference, British Museum, London, 1988, forthcoming.

WHITEHOUSE, D. and A.WILLIAMSON. "Sassanian Maritime Trade", *Iran* 11, 1973.

WHYBROW, P. ET AL "Fauna of Fossil Mammals from the Miocene of Saudi Arabia", *Nature* 274, 1978. "Dryopithecines from the Miocene of Saudi Arabia", *Nature* 274, 1978.

WILLIAMSON, A. "Hurmuz and the Trade of the Gulf in the 14th and 15th Centuries AD", *PSAS*, 1973.

WILSON, A.T. *The Persian Gulf*. Oxford, 1928.

WINDER, R. BAYLY *Saudi Arabia in the Nineteenth Century*. London, 1965.

WINSTONE, H.V.F. *Captain Shakespear*. London, 1976. *Leachman: O.C. Desert*. London, 1982.

WÜSTENFELD, F. *Bahrain und Jemama, nach Arabischen Geographen beschrieben*. Göttingen, 1874.

ZARINS, J. "Steatite Vessels in the Riyadh Museum", *Atlal* 2, 1978. "MAR-TU and the Land of Dilmun", *BTAA*, 1986. "Camel (C. dromedarius, C. bactrianus)", entry in *Anchor Bible Dictionary*, forthcoming.

ZARINS, J., A.S. MUGHANNUM, M.KAMAL "Excavations at Dhahran South – the Tumuli Field (208-92), 1983", *Atlal* 8, 1984.

ZWEMER, S.M. *Arabia: the Cradle of Islam*. New York, 1900.

Plans and maps of al-Hasa and the Eastern Province

Arabian Peninsula, 1:2,000,000. Director of Military Survey, Ministry of Defence, United Kingdom, 1973.

Hofuf, 1:1,000,000. D Survey, War Office and Air Ministry, London, 1963.

Al-Hufuf, 1:250,000, Sheet NG 39-10. Ministry of Petroleum and Mineral Resources, Air Survey Department, Riyadh 1983.

The Oasis of Al-Hasa 1951-1952. Compiled by F.S. Vidal. In back of *The Oasis of Al-Hasa* by F.S. Vidal, Dhahran 1955.

TPC H-6C. Tactical Pilotage Chart H-6C, Bahrain, Iran, Qatar, Saudi Arabia, United Arab Emirates, 1:500,000. Director of Military Survey, Ministry of Defence, United Kingdom 1985, revised 1987.

AR RUQTAH: Sheet 5942 I.

SAFWA: Sheet 5943 II.

RAS TANURA: Sheet 6043 III.

DHAHRAN: Sheet 6042 IV.

Maps at 1:50,000 showing Qatif Oasis, compiled in 1954. Army Map Service (AMLU), Corps of Engineers, US Army, Washington DC.

Index

A page number in **bold** denotes the page
on which an illustration appears.

TRANSLITERATION

In transliterating Arabic words and names, diacritical dots and long vowel indicators have been omitted. The definite article al- has been largely dispensed with, except for regional names such as al-Hasa and al-Qasim, and for certain place-names, such as al-Khobar, in conformity with popular expatriate usage. Proper names which are familiar to English-speaking readers in a certain form, such as Dhahran, Riyadh, Saud and Abdullah, even if strictly incorrect, are left in their conventional guise. Otherwise the basis of the transliteration system used is that in *Arabian Studies*.

The definite article al- should not be confused with the word Al in front of a name, with capital A and without a hyphen, which denotes "family of" or "clan of".

Glossary

'alim	(pl. *'ulama'*) learned scholars of religion and law, whose rulings form the basis of Islamic government.
badawi	member of a bedouin tribe
badu	collective plural of *badawi*; bedouin
barasti	palm frond dwelling
bisht	outer cloak worn by men
dikakah	sandy terrain well vegetated after rain
dirah	tribal territory, established annual migration in search of pasture
Ikhwan	literally "Brothers"; the name given to members of the bedouin settlement movement instigated by Ibn Saud c.1911. Its fighting men were instrumental in Ibn Saud's campaign to unify the Kingdom up until 1926.
'irq	(pl. *'uruq*) longitudinal sand-dunes, whose form aligns with the wind direction
ithl	tamarisk
jihad	religious struggle, holy war
jabal	hill, rock outcrop
nakhuda	boat captain
qanat	underground channel cut through the rock, tapping the water table, for irrigation and general water supply
qasr	(pl. *qusur*) fortified palace or house
rimal	sands, sand desert
sabkhah	salt flat, shallow saline lagoon
saluq	sweet, dry confection produced by boiling yellow dates
sambouk; ghanjah; baqqarah; shu'ai; boum; baghlah; battil; jalibut	types of fishing, pearling or trading boats
sanjak	the term used to define an administrative district or region under Ottoman rule: a subdivision of a vilayet, or province
shajar	perennial vegetation, as distinct from *'ushb*
shamal	dry, north-westerly wind, prevailing in summer
shashah	simple fishing vessel made from palm frond mid-ribs lashed together
tajir	merchant; pearl wholesaler
tawwash	small-scale pearl dealer
'ushb	annual vegetation, as distinct from *shajar*